To

Carmen

who is living

a new challenge

in her life

Here's what others are saying about
Hunger, Hunches, and Hustle . . .

"He is one of the world's great salespeople. I've sat with him in what I thought was an impossible selling situation and seen him work his magic. Now he has put the secrets of a lifetime of selling into a remarkable entertaining and well-written book. It's a must read, not only for salespeople and sales managers, but also for anyone who has ever wanted to get anyone to do anything."

—ROGER DAWSON, AUTHOR OF
SECRETS OF POWER NEGOTIATING

"Success and failure are a daily part of every salesperson's life. Many of us go through life never knowing why we succeed, or why we fail, therefore making it difficult to develop success patterns. I've found Bruce to be one of the most profound thinkers and analysts I have ever encountered. When he wins (and this is often), he analyzes precisely who said what to whom and is thus able to develop success methods. When he loses, he uses the same process to eliminate losing behaviors. That's what makes him one of the nation's top real estate teachers."

—HANK TRISLER, AUTHOR OF
NO BULL SELLING

"Bruce is a master salesperson and highly effective communicator who dynamically provides creative, insightful and exciting sales techniques with a practical approach."

—DAVE DOELEMAN, SENIOR INSTRUCTOR,
REALTORS NATIONAL MARKETING INSTITUTE

Hunger, Hunches, & Hustle

An Englishman's 40 Years of Selling Experience and Misadventures in California Real Estate

Bruce T. Mulhearn

Grasmere Press
CERRITOS, CALIFORNIA 90703

First printing 2002
Second printing 2005

ISBN 0-9708089-3-3

LCCN 2001131683

DEDICATION

This book is dedicated to my first real estate manager and mentor Ben Hinkle, from whom I learned so much. Ben's favorite line was, "Enthusiasm is knowledge on fire," and he represented it so well. The sincere smile, the aura of excitement that surrounded him with the adrenaline that pumped through his system, sparked the best in those who were guided by his leadership. His never-say-die attitude inspired me never to give up my quest to be the best I could be.

Ben was a milkman before he got into the real estate business in the 1950s. It was a difficult transition for him. In the first few months he fell behind in his house mortgage and car payments. Then a blessing came. He sold two homesites for which he would make 10 percent commission on the $20,000 sale. He was ecstatic until he received a phone call from his manager—the $1,000 deposit check Ben received had bounced. Ben found himself at the lowest point in his real estate career, but he resolved to turn that negative experience around. His choice was clear. Did he continue with his vision or did he return to the security and obscurity of his old employment? There was no place to go in the real estate business but up, which he did. Ben became a multimillionaire.

CONTENTS

Foreword ix

A Confession xi

◆ Say What You Mean and Mean What You Say 1

◆ I Never Missed a Game 3

◆ Fatigue and Hadrian's Wall 5

◆ The Morris Minor Truck 7

◆ The Home Came With The Mural 9

◆ No, Sonny, You're Going to Give Me a Ride! 11

◆ The Fabled Taste of a Kentucky Smoked Ham 14

◆ So He Broke the Rules 16

◆ It Takes All Kinds of People 19

◆ The Bird Sang 21

◆ In His Day, Everyone Wore Hats 25

◆ We Wrote It on a Paper Towel 28

◆ Mrs. Eveready 30

◆ I Enjoy a Good Bet 32

◆ The Second Battle of Britain 34

◆ Plowing the 40 Acres 36

◆ You'll Like What I Did Next 38

◆ You Have the Potential of Being a Fine Speaker 41

◆ You Have an Insurmountable Impediment 44

◆ That's One Small Step for Man,
One Giant Leap for Mankind 45

◆ Josko Pulled Out a Little Red Book 47

◆ Home Is a Very Potent Force 49

◆ Kerosene Lamps "Shed Light on the Occasion" 52

◆ Where Are You Calling From? 54

◆ What Had I Learned to This Point? 56

◆ My Friend Karl 59

◆ Sometime Next Year 61

◆ The Jigsaw Puzzle 63

◆ It Took One Phone Call 65

◆ The Magic of an Orange 67

◆ The Concorde 69

◆ Bussing Tables 71

◆ Open a Cage and a Bird Will Fly Away 73

◆ Be the Best You Can Be 75

◆ Do We Really Have to Listen to
Englebert Humperdinck? 77

◆ Eradio 80

◆ There Must Be a Mistake 82

◆ Roy Rogers 84

◆ Tim Can Marinate Filet Mignon 86

◆ Variations of White, Burgundy, and
Brown at the Class Reunion 88

◆ Lost in Chicago With a Jamaican Cabby 90

◆ San Jacinto 92

◆ Do We Judge a Book by Its Cover? 96

◆ One Hundred Dollars Per Minute 98

◆ Aunt Evelyn 100

◆ Wanna Buy a Book? Wanna Catch a Fish? 102

◆ The Skiing Experience 104

◆ Embracing Rejection 107

◆ So What Can I Pass On to Others? 110

FOREWORD

This book is about inspiring people and events told in the context of Bruce Mulhearn's life experiences. These unique and entertaining episodes from his accomplishments and misadventures as a salesman will help you on your own journey toward greater success and satisfaction.

There are some amusing tales about how to compete and still have fun in the business of real estate, as well as some harrowing stories about how to deal with adversity when business expectations turn sour.

Bruce has traveled quite a road since his childhood in northern England, where his first sales job was with his father when Bruce was just eight years old. He sold Gleamy, the British version of Clorox bleach, door-to-door and soon had his first lesson in sales. He learned how to overcome rejection, anxiety, and stress, and how to make customers out of people whose first response was negative.

Still in his teens, he moved to New Zealand, where he worked in a tanning factory by day and in a fast-food restaurant by night. Bruce arrived in the United States in 1958 and two years later, at the age of 21, obtained his real estate license.

A stint in the U.S. Army—along with selling and buying property; building a major real estate, mortgage, and escrow firm; raising a family; developing land; and weathering the business turmoil from the 1960s to the 1990s—make up the Bruce Mulhearn story.

He learned the importance of creating balance in one's life. Being "all work" is an easy rut in which to fall. It cannot only make you unhappy—it can kill you. Eating well and exercising properly is vital. So is a healthy belief in yourself and your abilities.

It is also important to be thoroughly professional—from how you look to how you behave—in the business setting. Attitude, self-discipline, goals, and sales skills are all important.

When Bruce started in business, he didn't know much about what he was doing. He did, however, have the common sense to become a willing and eager student.

Each day he learns what he has to do to present the best in himself to the world.

Danielle Kennedy

A CONFESSION

As a firm believer in not procrastinating, I violated my own rule in letting my manuscript collect dust for months at a time. Over the past two or three years I would spasmodically pick up my rough notes and frustrate my assistant, Mary McEntee, by having her attempt one more time to put it all together. I finally realized I was not practicing what I preach to others: today, not tomorrow. Just do it.

It has taken me a long time to reduce the thoughts in this book to writing. Wrestling it to completion reminds me of one of my favorite stories.

A young man decided to go back to his home state to find his roots. He found the homestead, now surrounded with overgrown weeds. It lay completely abandoned. He'd come a long way, so he tore down the boards from one of the windows, climbed inside, and found himself in the dining room in which stood a wooden table and chairs covered with dust. He recalled his childhood with his brothers and sisters eating their meals.

He noticed an old tweed jacket on one chair, shook off the dust, and put it on. It was his and still fit! He reached through the pockets and found a claim check for a pair of shoes he'd put in the cobbler shop 20 years ago. Was the repair shop still open? Is the old cobbler still alive?

Going to the village, he found the shop—paint peeling from the walls, duct tape holding the windows together. Inside was an old man, now stooped over and with a gray beard. He threw the claim check on the table and said, "I've come to pick up my shoes." The old man didn't blink an eye, slowly picked up the claim check, shuffled to the back room, came back and said, "They'll be ready next Tuesday."

We live in a world of procrastination. We all have Tuesdays in our lives. I finally faced mine.

SAY WHAT YOU MEAN AND MEAN WHAT YOU SAY

"The life of children, as much as that of intemperate men,
is wholly governed by their desires."
—ARISTOTLE

Preparing our thoughts before we voice them is so important. It also pays to put our thoughts into writing before we express them. It lessens the chance that they will be misread or misinterpreted.

Selling bleach door-to-door with my father brought me into contact with a delightful woman named Mrs. Laws. She was one of my favorite customers.

Every Saturday morning when I called on Mrs. Laws she had a piece of fruit for me. Food rationing in post–World War II England was finally coming to an end, but it was still very difficult to obtain fruit. I didn't even taste a banana until I was seven. It had been tough enough having oil tankers import oil to Britain, never mind the lower priority items such as produce.

Although the average customer used a bottle of our bleach once every two weeks, every week when I showed up at Mrs. Laws', she always replaced her empty bottle. I swear she must have poured half a bottle down the toilet just to buy another one from me.

I started wondering about getting this fresh fruit each week. I wondered if Mrs. Laws could afford it. I speculated she was doing it out of a sense of having started a routine she felt she had to keep up.

One Saturday morning when Mrs. Laws offered me an apple, I said, "No thank you, Mrs. Laws." I never again received fruit from her. I realized afterwards I had not thought out a correct approach to

1

the problem. Whether she was offended because I turned the fruit down or grateful because it had been difficult for her to obtain it in the first place, I would never know.

The result was not what I wanted and it may not have been what she wanted. What I should have said was, "Mrs. Laws, I really do appreciate your giving me fruit every week, and I hope I'm not putting you out. I like it very much, but if there comes a time when you don't have any fruit for me, please don't feel badly about it. I'm grateful for whatever I receive."

◆　◆　◆　◆　◆

*If I had been able to tell her what I
really felt, Mrs. Laws could then have made a
decision based on what she wanted.
Perhaps we both lost. I had not properly explored
her needs and desires.*

I NEVER
MISSED A GAME

"They are able because they think they are able."
—VIRGIL

As a young boy in England, I loved to play soccer. The problem was that the games were played on Saturday afternoons, which was when my father needed me to work with him selling bleach.

One morning I asked, "Dad, can I play soccer?"

"Yes, you can, Bruce. Here is what we'll do." He built a cart and on it put a box that could hold 12 bottles of the bleach. He dropped me off in his van a mile and a half from home with the promise, "When you have sold all 12 bottles, you can play."

I never missed a game. My urge to play overcame my fear of rejection. This was based on my belief that the reward was greater than my emotional risk.

When I became older, I began to understand this tremendous fear of rejection from which most of us suffer. Recognizing the fear and overcoming it made selling much easier.

In selling bleach, I normally serviced regular customers at the beginning of each day and prospected for new customers in the afternoon. I put off the tough part until the very end of the day, enjoying the pleasant part of my day first—meeting my regular customers.

However, this fear of rejection mounted as the day went on until it became monumental. One morning I decided to reverse the procedure and prospect at the beginning of the day when I was fresh and the fear hadn't built up. Changing priorities made me extremely effective.

◆ ◆ ◆ ◆ ◆

The most important priorities are
usually the least pleasant.
They should always be completed first.

FATIGUE AND
HADRIAN'S WALL

"The man who believes he can do it is probably right, and so is the man who believes he can't."
—LAWRENCE J. PETER

When we start out on an adventure, we usually begin with a great deal of optimism, enthusiasm, and energy. There are also fear of failure and intimidation by the unknown. The real effort to succeed has to occur in the long and often tedious haul when the newness has worn off. Then the going gets tougher.

When I was 15, a couple of friends and I decided to cycle from Newcastle-Upon-Tyne to Carlisle and back. Carlisle is near the Scottish border 57 miles from Newcastle-Upon-Tyne. The highway runs parallel to the 70-mile-long Hadrian's Wall. The wall was built 2,000 years ago by a Roman general, Hadrian, to keep the Celtic clans from raiding England.

We took off at 7:00 A.M. on a beautiful summer Sunday morning. In the north England summertime, it grows dark at 10:00 P.M. This gave us extra hours of daylight to get home. All three of us were full of energy and high spirits. The first 30 miles were a breeze; over halfway to our destination we were feeling strong. If you are goal-oriented and are over the hump to your first objective, you just don't give up. We pushed on.

Ten miles from Carlisle we began to flag, but the prize of being so close was the only encouragement needed. At 2:30 we arrived, tired but happy. It was the halfway point of the overall journey. We rewarded ourselves with fried eggs, mushy peas, and chips, the tastiest yet most inappropriate food to digest. Sitting down to eat was a mistake. Getting up was sheer torture. Our legs shook and our behinds were chafed. The rest and food intake nevertheless revived our spirits and we pedaled hard on the comeback trail. It seemed much longer than the way we'd come. The scenery was now familiar and boring as we knew what was around the next bend.

I punctured my tire. Although we were able to change it in 30 minutes, the delay made my friends impatient. At about 4:30, a remarkable change came over me. Perhaps it was my body chemistry—endorphins flooding the bloodstream. My bicycle and I became one. The aches and pains vanished. I became a robot without feeling, on automatic pilot traveling fast. This condition lasted for almost four hours.

At dusk I lost my concentration. I failed to negotiate a bend and took a spill. The scrapes and bruises made me angry but I was able to convert this negative emotion into a thrashing of the bike pedals. It kept me moving. Five miles from home, my father found us. He had been cruising in his large Morris van, worried we had been involved in an accident. We piled gratefully into the rear of the vehicle.

The next day at school, I was in agony. Everything hurt. I felt like the bicycle seat had become a permanent attachment and couldn't sit comfortably anywhere. My walk was a shuffle. In spite of it all, I was extremely proud of the achievement.

In reflection, the message is clear. Never give up, never ever give up. Whatever the odds, you can overcome them if you have confidence in yourself.

◆　◆　◆　◆　◆

Exhaustion can take a backseat
depending on your perception of how close
you are to your goal.

THE MORRIS MINOR TRUCK

"Common sense is perhaps the most equally divided, but surely the most underemployed talent in the world."
—CHRISTIANE COLLANGE

When I was 16, my father allowed me to have my own door-to-door business route. My first automobile was a second-hand Morris truck that had belonged to the British Post Office. The vehicle had rubberized fenders. My father told me he wouldn't stand in the way of my driving. The fenders underscored his message. If the fender hit any object, I could reverse and the fender would bounce right back.

We expanded our bleach route to include soaps and carpet cleaner, and delivered replacement orders every two weeks.

One morning I had a flat tire. There was a spare but no jack, which caused me to grumble about my father's incompetence. (How easy it is to blame others for our own lack of preparation!) Angered by the delay and frustrated that the wasted time was eating into my commissions, I wrestled for a solution.

I decided to continue canvassing the block. I asked customers if they could lend me a jack. Eventually, I found a woman who allowed me to borrow her husband's jack. Blinded by impatience and the need to meet my daily goals, I replaced the wheel but only hand tightened the lug bolts. (Haste makes waste!)

At the precise moment I slowed to pass a school, the wheel left the truck. As I hung onto the steering wheel for dear life, the vehicle swerved from side to side and sparks flew. The truck came to a screeching halt in a cloud of dust. The stench of sodium hydrochloride from the bleach permeated the air as it rose from the back. There were broken bottles scattered everywhere. Surrounded by a crowd of giggling kids at recess, I felt humiliation, guilt, and anger.

At a nearby telephone booth, I called home to voice my frustrations to my father. My tirade began with me blaming him for his thoughtlessness in leaving me stranded. Why was the truck so illequipped? Dad listened patiently to my raving until my venting subsided. Quietly responding with a classic alternate-choice close, he said, "Well, Bruce, I appreciate how you feel. As I see it, you've two options. You can come home for the balance of the day if you don't feel like working, or I can send you out another truck with a new supply of bleach so you can continue. Which would you prefer?"

Something inside told me I didn't want to quit. "Send me another truck," I said. Later I had time to examine what had happened that morning and apologized. My father had converted my frustration into a valuable lesson. When verbally attacked, our reaction is to fight back, to trade bullets. Instead, my father had chosen to listen. He used common sense and allowed me to express my misguided anger. It gave me time to unwind, and he gave me a reasonable solution. It worked!

For the balance of that day, I was transformed. I was behind and challenged and able to sell more bleach in less time than on any other day. People just couldn't say "no" that day. The vibrations were right.

◆ ◆ ◆ ◆ ◆

My hostility had almost consumed me.
Now this pent-up, negative energy had been
converted into a highly positive force for
achievement. This transformation was a conscious
effort to compensate.

THE HOME CAME WITH
THE MURAL

*"He [Benjamin Disraeli] is a self-made man
and worships his creator."*

—JOHN BRIGHT

It was December 1960. My parents were about to purchase their first home in the United States. I'd been studying for my real estate license and had become knowledgeable about things like alluvium soil, riparian rights, and metes and bounds. I was hot stuff. There was no room for humility in my untried mind. Perhaps I was at the first level of learning—the unconscious incompetent stage where you don't know that you don't know.

T. K. Bass was the real estate broker showing homes to Mom and Dad. He was a professional and exhibited it through supreme self-confidence. As the 20-year-old family real estate expert, I went along as my parents' guardian angel. There was a beautiful little Spanish stucco home that had recently been placed on the market by T. K. It was an early December evening and the air was chilly as we knocked on the front door. T. K. stood strategically behind us. As the door opened, a draft of warm air hit us in the face.

It beckoned us inside. We waited for an invitation, which didn't come. As our eyes became accustomed to the gloom, we saw a couple seated on a couch at the far end of the living room. One of the two shadowy forms got up and stretched over to a light switch on the wall. He flicked it on. The whole room was transformed. Ultraviolet lights stretching from floor to ceiling on both sides of the room illuminated an iridescent mural of two men in a small boat fishing on a

9

lake's placid waters. The background was green meadows, pine trees, snow-capped peaks, and fleecy white clouds in a deep blue sky.

Mom's mouth dropped open in utter amazement. An Italian painter had completed this work of art in earlier times. The commanding voice of T. K. startled us. He ordered us to follow him and like sheep we did—not into the home but across the front lawn sidewalk street until we reached the opposite curb.

On his command, we faced the home, shivering with cold. As if by rehearsal, the drapes shielding the interior were drawn back from the arched Spanish window that dominated the front exterior wall. Mom's eyes were transfixed by that painting on the living room wall.

Mom bought the mural that evening. The home happened to be attached to it. It had two bedrooms not three, which we originally thought we needed. There was a little annex bedroom and half bath in the garage—my punishment. That became my part of the home until I married. Some expert, me!

Recalling that experience, I have to salute T. K. Bass. I can only imagine what he told the owners when he put the property on the market for sale. Perhaps they even rehearsed the episodes—turn on the light switch, have the prospects walk across the street, then open the drapes. He was a showman.

Mom and Dad paid $17,500 for the home, even though the FHA appraisal came in at $14,500. They gladly paid $3,000 more than the appraisal. It was the lake scene that did it.

◆   ◆   ◆   ◆   ◆

If I had asked my mother if she
bought with her head or her heart, I believe
she would have responded,
"With my head," not willing to admit that
her emotions got the better of her. Like most of us,
she bought with emotion, not logic.

NO, SONNY, YOU'RE GOING TO GIVE ME A RIDE!

*"The world turns aside to let any man pass
who knows whither he is going."*
—DAVID S. JORDAN

While working for the Apple Valley Building and Development Company in 1961, I was proud to be the top salesperson out of a staff of 175. It wasn't that I was the smartest—I just worked harder.

The average salesperson would go 100 miles to Apple Valley resort once or twice a week with customers, but I created a formula that allowed up to four trips a day. Every time I sold a homesite to a prospect, I'd ask if he would like to obtain a real estate license and help me. Quite a number did on a part-time basis, hence the increased number of trips with these assistants.

When I traveled from Los Angeles to Apple Valley with customers, my company gave me a steak breakfast and $25. It took two hours to tour the valley and I sometimes completed four trips on both Saturday and Sunday with my agents shuttling in my next prospects. Through with one customer, I dropped him off and another one appeared. A team effort with specific roles for each team member can be extremely productive. It was much more efficient and effective than just making one trip a day.

One morning I traveled to the city of Cudahy in my 1957 DeSoto, a car that looked like a spaceship. Gas was 22 cents a gallon. Bruce Porter, the owner of a Flying A gas station there, was a possible investor in land in the high desert. Wanting to make an appointment

11

with him to show Apple Valley, I waited in his office as I filled my car with fuel. Fifteen minutes later, I had made the appointment and returned to my car.

A large dissipated woman in her mid-50s with ebony black hair and contrasting white roots was sitting in the front seat passenger side. Looking around, I could see no other cars in the parking lot. Timidly, I tapped on the window of my car. She rolled down the window and smiled. All three of her teeth showed. She asked, "What do you want, young man?"

I replied, "Ma'am, you're sitting in the wrong car."

She grinned again and said, "No, sonny, you're going to give me a ride."

How was I going to remove her? I finally said, "Well, which way are you going?"

"North," she replied. I had wanted to go south; however, without further question, I went north. She had used the physical action close—first by getting into my car, then by refusing to get out.

Her name was Jackie Trivasano. She would have fit right in as one of the bizarre characters in the old musical, *Guys and Dolls*. She told me she carried a small Derringer between extremely large breasts and had with her a miniature, bad-tempered Chihuahua, who ate nothing but fried chicken.

Twenty minutes later we reached her destination, a run-down motel. She said, "Bruce, I'm moving today." I thought to myself, *I bet you're being evicted*. In any case, I spent the next three hours helping her move. When we finished, she said, "Bruce, you've been very kind. Give me some of your business cards. I'll send some customers your way." I thought, *That will never happen*, but I obliged her, gave her my cards, and left.

Much to my surprise, I received calls from a never-ending stream of people who had been directed to me by Jackie. I created sales from these referrals.

Jackie was a diamond in the rough who perhaps could have been an outstanding salesperson. She had many of the necessary attributes. She reached out all the time and ignored rejection. Yet she was drifting from motel to motel because she had no direction. She had no goals and wasn't very happy. I was too young to guide her. I was going through transformations as I learned the sales business. Training her never crossed my mind.

Jackie and I stayed in touch for a number of years. She'd call me on her birthday—collect, of course—and I would send her a bunch of violets. One year she didn't and I knew she was gone.

Upon reflection, I'm sure with maturity I could have suggested to Jackie to consider going in the right direction. By observing her lack of it, I believe it compelled me to have more direction. She demonstrated the consequences of being adrift. I regret not doing more for her now than I did, but would it have made any change in her life?

◆　◆　◆　◆　◆

As teachers, all we can do is point the way
by opening the door. It's up to
each student to go through that same door.

THE FABLED TASTE
OF A KENTUCKY
SMOKED HAM

*"Thinking is the hardest work there is, which is the
probable reason why so few engage in it."*
—HENRY FORD

Allen was a superstar salesperson, a consistent award winner. As a newcomer to land sales, I wanted to spend enough time with him to unlock some of his secrets. He was so busy it wasn't easy to pin him down. We finally met for breakfast. He told me that much of his business was by referral and he gave an example why.

One evening, Allen was returning to his office with a young couple from Kentucky who had just bought property from him. They were enthusiastic but nervous about their decision. Allen knew that the first 48 hours after a purchase were critical. Friends and relatives could easily sway buyers into believing that they may have made the wrong choice. We've all experienced buying a new car and then being told by others we should have bought a different model.

Allen was convinced the property was right for this couple. He always believed in building extensive rapport with his customers. He would probe into their backgrounds, leaving no stone unturned. In his conversations, he offered little, asked lots of questions, and listened. This couple had been in California for less than a year and they were homesick.

They reminisced with Allen about a little farm factory in their hometown that sold cured smoked hams. Nothing in the world was as delicious. They couldn't find a place in California that stocked them. Allen listened intently.

Upon arriving home, Allen made some long-distance phone calls. By air express the next day, he had a special package delivered to his office. It contained a carefully packed ham from that small farm. The total cost of the gift was $28. (That was a long time ago!)

That same evening, Allen rang the doorbell of his Kentucky customers. When the woman answered, he handed her the gift and urged her and her husband to open it. She squealed with delight at the contents. She worked as a teller in a local bank. For at least the next six months, everyone who came to her window learned about how wonderful Allen was. She had a stack of his business cards. He kept track of his direct referrals and he calculated that he earned 28 referrals in commission fees from that one source.

One might criticize Allen, claiming the gift was purely a manipulation, but no one would debate the fact that he had his awareness antenna in place. When he gave the gift, he did not realize that he would be rewarded so handsomely. His primary goal had been to thank his customers for the business and reassure them that their decision had been correct.

◆　◆　◆　◆　◆

*Success does not come by accident.
It takes a thinking, creative salesperson
to achieve Allen's results.*

SO HE BROKE
THE RULES

*"To exist is to change, to change is to mature, to mature
is to go on creating oneself endlessly."*
—HENRY BERGSON

Showing vacant homesites in Apple Valley was both an art and a science. The air was clean out in the California desert 100 miles from Los Angeles and three thousand feet above sea level. Friends teased that there was absolutely nothing there except jackrabbits and Joshua trees. This was definitely true in the 1940s, but in the 1960s, because of the efforts of Newton Bass—a developer who built an airport, golf course, bank, post office, and a very attractive hotel equipped with spas, a swimming pool, and many other amenities—this had changed.

I drove 50,000 miles during my first year of selling; gas was 22 cents a gallon. My 1957 DeSoto had air conditioning and a front bench seat.

Pulling in front of the homesite I wanted to show, I would immediately point out its size, normally a minimum of 100 by 150 feet. This was literally three times the size of the tiny Los Angeles 50- by 100-foot lots. I always referred to Los Angeles as "down below." It implied that at the end of our day we would again descend into hell—the Los Angeles Basin.

It was not unusual to find beautiful custom-built homes on the same street as the homesites I showed. If these homes were close by, I would take a short side trip to demonstrate a before-and-after view. Looking at a vacant desert lot with only Joshua trees and sagebrush was not the most inspiring sight.

I would pull up next to a beautifully landscaped home. First, I'd ask my guests to look at the vacant desert lot across the street. I would ask, "In looking at that vacant homesite, could you ever imagine having the ability to grow anything?" I would dramatically turn my head to the opposite side of the street and look with great intensity at the landscaped home. "Isn't this an amazing contrast? All it requires is a little water." I'd go on to say, "When we reach your vacant homesite, I want you to remember what I've just shown you."

First, the physical action close. Jumping out of my car, I'd run around to the passenger side, throw open the door, and enthusiastically say, "Follow me." My guests would quickly obey as my big, slow, measured steps took us to the very back of the homesite. I'd turn to face the majestic Sierras 40 miles to the west.

Gulping in a breath of fresh desert air, I'd point out Mount Baldy, 10,000 feet above sea level, usually covered with snow at least nine months out of the year. I'd talk about the beautiful contrasts in scenery and reach down and pick up a handful of soil, slowly sifting it through my fingers. I'd ask my guests to recall the view of the landscaped home and use their imaginations on this homesite. "Simply add water to the earth and vegetation will grow."

One morning while in the middle of a presentation, I noticed what looked like a 100-foot long black Cadillac sedan pull up in a cloud of dust behind my car. It belonged to Larry Wilson, who missed his calling as a TV evangelist. He had oodles of charisma and a deep baritone voice.

I smiled to myself. Even though Larry was a formidable competitor and one of the top salespeople in our company, I had the benefit of time in my favor. The company policy on showing vacant homesites had me 15 minutes ahead of Larry and his presentation. I also knew my buyers were ecstatic about the lot. Watching Larry out of the corner of my eye, I waited for him to jump enthusiastically out of his car and follow the company routine. It didn't happen!

He began waving his arms excitedly in the air, pointing in my direction while making dramatic gestures. Suddenly, the Cadillac reversed and with screeching tires took off in a cloud of desert dust, speeding in the direction of the developer's main offices. The light went on. Larry was using me to sell the homesite to his customers. He had improvised, ignoring the "rules" of the game. "How unfair!" I self-righteously mumbled.

I looked quickly at my prospects and almost shouted, "Would you like to own this homesite?" There was no more direct way to ask for the order. After the startled look left their eyes, they said, "Yes." I said, "Follow me," and charged off at a fast trot to my DeSoto, my breathless guests in tow.

In hot pursuit, we raced 70 miles per hour across the desert road to catch up. We were two minutes too late. As we marched into the office, the loudspeaker was blaring out the name of Larry and his buyers. The whole world knew they had bought that homesite.

My buyers ended up with another lot that day. It was not quite the one they wanted, but they bought it for less than the one they'd expected to purchase.

After recovering from the initial shock of being outsmarted, I recognized the value of what I had learned that day: Larry changed the routine to fit the conditions.

◆　◆　◆　◆　◆

You are allowed to break the rules
provided it's legal and ethical.

IT TAKES ALL KINDS
OF PEOPLE

*"Not to be worked by anyone's hand, to be no one's man,
to draw one's principles, one's feelings from no one else,
this is the rarest thing I have seen."*
—NICOLAS CHAMFORT

As a trainee working with the Apple Valley Building and Development Company in the 1960s, I was not allowed to close sales. The customer was turned over to a marketing vice president after I'd given them a tour. There were six vice presidents with varied personalities and backgrounds. Each tour guide determined which personality would bond most readily with the customer and have the best opportunity to complete the transaction.

There was Glen. He looked like Robert Redford in a sequined cowboy suit. He reflected the image of Apple Valley as an equestrian paradise. Single and handsome, the professional career women were guided to his office. Looking back, this was an extremely sexist manipulation.

Customers who were blue-collar workers were generally introduced to Ben, who was down to earth and very enthusiastic. He'd been a door-to-door milkman before entering the real estate business.

Engineers met Bill, who also piloted and maintained the company plane. Bill talked nuts and bolts with engineers, operating logically out of the left side of his brain.

Accountants, CPAs, and architects met Jack. He was also the company controller and possessed an analytical mind—strictly a bottom-line guy.

Any foreign-born customer with even the slightest accent ended up in Herman's office—a huge German from Berlin. With his European background, he could identify with almost everyone from a foreign land.

Which one was the most appropriate for the customer at hand? There was such diversity in these deal makers. Although competitors, they worked cohesively to maximize their individual qualities combined with the information that came from the trained tour guides.

What a learning experience it was for any young career-minded salesperson to watch each executive close sales using his unique approach.

◆　◆　◆　◆　◆

*In studying the performance of other professionals
who have cultivated their success with
honed skills and sheer experience, we can emulate
the strengths they offer and guard against
their weaknesses, which remain.*

THE BIRD SANG

"He's a poor loser. Did you ever hear of a rich one?"
—ANONYMOUS

Competition is the spice of life. There are three types of competition—self, between individuals, and teams.

In my early career, I had my real estate license with a small agency in Bellflower. One morning I walked into the office and my two major in-house competitors, Jerry Lanting and Gary Olson, grabbed me by both arms. They tauntingly escorted me to the blackboards, which always contained production figures for the month to date. Both had just taken white chalk and scratched new sales on the blackboards. It was the beginning of the month; my name wasn't yet on the board.

Smiling lamely, I congratulated them on their productivity. However, they had triggered my inner demons. Did I want to be second or third best that month?

Immediately I decided I wasn't going home until I'd scratched something on the blackboard. In later years, I used the example of the depth of my intensity by communicating to audiences, "If someone said to you, you're going to have a sale on the blackboard today or be shot at midnight, would you have a sale?" The answer is obvious—"Yes"—even if you had to sell an unneeded home to your mother.

My humble 1960 Plymouth Valiant beckoned. (I'd just been released from my nonpaying career as a two-year draftee in the army.) Jumping into the car to go prospecting, I reconsidered. Why drive somewhere? It only took extra time. My minutes should be used to meet prospects.

21

So I walked down Bixby Street knocking on doors. At the seventh home I met a young couple surrounded by boxes. With the door ajar, I asked, "Are you interested in selling your home?"

"No."

I asked why, and they answered, "We are renting." They were moving. I asked if they would be interested in purchasing a home but quickly determined they did not have the financial ability to do so even if they wanted.

I asked who owned the home they were renting. They told me it was Mr. and Mrs. Birdsong. It turned out they were just around the corner on Walnut Street. Running to the house and knocking on Mr. Birdsong's door, I noticed too late a "No Soliciting—Day Sleeper" sign by the door.

There was the sound of shuffling, grunting, and wheezing behind the door. It was pulled open by a huge bleary-eyed fellow in a robe, wearing a day's growth of beard. He asked why I was standing at his door. Apologizing for disturbing his sleep, I told him that his tenant on Bixby Street was moving and, "I wonder if you'd be interested in putting the property on the market for sale?"

He asked me to come in. The timing couldn't have been better, he said. He'd been thinking about selling. We sat down and talked and I found him both sophisticated and intimidating. He would give me 48 hours in which to sell the house; otherwise, he'd rent it. Although taught to list a property for 120 days, I was desperate for a transaction that day and agreed.

The prior day, I'd received a phone call from Mr. DeVries, a Dutch carpenter looking for fixer-uppers. Mr. Birdsong's house fit the description. I dashed back to the office to telephone Mr. DeVries; he was going to be the first to see the home. In the middle of dialing, I hung up. Why not go out, unannounced, to persuade Mr. DeVries in person instead of making a telephone appointment? It's easy to get rid of a voice; it's difficult to get rid of a body.

Upon arrival, Mr. DeVries was working on a cabinet. The machines were humming as I said, "Good morning, Mr. DeVries, I'm Bruce Mulhearn. I talked with you yesterday about a fixer-upper. I apologize for not making an appointment, but I have a brand-new listing that you should see immediately. No one else knows about it. Could you please come with me to my car? I'll have you back in 30 minutes."

DeVries had a choice. He could tell me to go fly a kite or shut off the machinery. He pulled the plug and followed me to the car. When I climbed in, I apologized for my enthusiasm and broke the speed limit going back to Bellflower.

We inspected the house in less than ten minutes. With a quick in-and-out inspection, he said that he didn't want to buy the house for $14,500—this was a long time ago, remember—but he would make an offer of $13,750. I asked if he would at least meet the seller halfway. He said, "Bring the property price to $14,000 and we'll do business." I dropped him off and was heading back to see Mr. Birdsong when I decided to go back to my office and research the most recent comparable sales. Frankly, I felt that $14,000 was a fair price, but I wanted some recent sales to back me up.

I went over to Mr. Birdsong with my comparable sales, having rehearsed a "fight story" to use if he rejected the offer. If you write up an offer too quickly, the seller thinks that you've underpriced the property. If you don't sell within 120 days, he thinks you've abandoned him.

After a long discussion, he finally agreed to a counteroffer of $14,250. I dashed back to Mr. DeVries, not knowing quite what to tell him. After a bit of talk, he agreed to $14,250 and added with a Cheshire grin, "I knew you could do it!"

I couldn't wait to get back to the office. My competitive instincts in full gear, I rushed into the office at 4 o'clock on that afternoon. I was alone, scratching my transaction on the blackboard. Then I made two phone calls—one each to Jerry and Gary. My script? "I'm sorry you're home, it's such a great day to sell. I wanted you to know I just put a double ender on the blackboard—unlike yours, it was both my listing and my sale." Revenge is sweet. This was just the beginning of the month.

The month turned out to be a record-producing month for all three of us. We competed all month to beat each other in what had become our game. It was fun, cohesive, and highly stimulating.

◆ ◆ ◆ ◆ ◆

*Do the best you can, with whatever
you have, wherever you are. A combination
of determination and talent.*

IN HIS DAY, EVERYONE WORE HATS

*"One difference between savagery and civilization is
a little courtesy. There's no telling what a
lot of courtesy would do."*
—CULLEN HIGHTOWER

E. C. Hill, a real estate agent during the 1940s, once told me that he always liked to show property when the lights were on—particularly if the house was empty. When he showed a vacant home, he always removed his hat as a sign of respect. A subtle gesture, not unlike tipping your hat when meeting a lady, he believed the buyers would be less critical of the home if his head were dutifully uncovered, anticipating corresponding warm feelings by his prospects. He lowered his voice—as if in church—as another gesture.

How people relate to you is based on the conscious and unconscious statements you make about yourself. Small courtesy tactics in the negotiating process can make all the difference.

Our delivery system is central to the marketing plan. Three areas of immense importance are:

- Our automobiles
- Our clothes
- Our desks

My first automobile cost me a number of transactions. It was a manual transmission, two-door Plymouth Valiant, a legacy from my draftee days in the army. Customers were continually cramped into the backseat and climbing in and out was a physical battle. The only redeeming factor was that I kept the car exceptionally clean.

The image I projected was unsatisfactory—the car said "economy." I had convinced myself it was all I could afford. That miserable excuse for a mobile office made me want to take it to the nearest wrecking yard to have the pleasure of watching it being crushed into a small rectangular box.

Finally, I decided I could no longer afford to keep this "affordable" car; I took a risk and purchased a beautiful two-year-old Chrysler New Yorker. It was big and spacious with luxurious leather seating and four doors—a delight to drive. No longer a chore to show property, everyone was relaxed, which led to less fatigue, creating a better mood for business. The Chrysler exuded success and that feeling rubbed off on me. It was my responsibility to match the image of my vehicle. What a refreshing difference; I had created a subliminal message that helped my clients buy.

An associate, Bill Duffey, was a prime example of the use of this philosophy. He and his wife Doris became a very wealthy couple, specializing in first-time home buyers. In the early 1970s, the average sale was $20,000, and it was not unusual for them to sell 15 homes in one month. Their record was nine homes in one weekend and 29 properties in 30 days. Salespeople questioned why he drove new, expensive cars. Some believed the Duffeys' beautiful car would make buyers resent them, and discourage first-time buyers from purchasing.

Bill's point of view was that buyers like dealing with winners, not losers. To be a winner, you have to look like one; he and Doris were living proof their plan worked. Bill Duffey was a great advocate of displaying the success image. He was rarely seen without an attractive coat, tie, and slacks. His shoes were always impeccably clean. Doris wore conservative but stylish women's suits and dresses.

An attorney friend in Century City specializes in the development and acquisition of banking institutions. He is a very bright and talented man; however, his one drawback is the first impression clients have when they visit his office. It makes me shudder every time I go there and I'm a friend! Papers piled everywhere, case files bulging out of cardboard boxes, building blueprints strewn here and there. His desk—the centerpiece of his office environment—looks like a disaster area. How much "stuff" can be piled on one small rectangular piece of expensive wood? This antique must have cost a fortune, but you'd never know it—a mystery left unseen by the mountains of pulp. The way a desk looks—how neat and clean it is, how efficiently it's arranged—can have a profound effect on how quickly issues can be resolved.

When he's teased about the mess, he just shrugs his shoulders and says he's going to correct the problem. But when? For a man who normally doesn't procrastinate, his workstation is his Achilles' heel. How many clients has it cost him over the years? He is still very successful, but things could probably be better. A clean desk could increase his income, make life easier, and make clients less uneasy.

In a book by Mark McCormack, Hollywood's Lew Wasserman would purportedly sweep through the MCA offices in the late evening and throw paperwork he found on anyone's desk into the wastebasket. The next day the offended executives would be told, "If you can't get it done before you leave, then it's not worth doing."

This was Wasserman's way of making employees aware of how they were using their time. A number of people who have met me late in the day have joked, "You must not be busy—there isn't a single piece of paper on your desk."

◆　◆　◆　◆　◆

On a subconscious level, our body language,
dress code, and personal surroundings register more
eloquently than any words we utter.
They must coincide. Who you are speaks so loud
I can't hear a word you say.

WE WROTE IT ON A PAPER TOWEL

*"Good judgment comes with experience.
But experience comes with bad judgment."*

—ANONYMOUS

It doesn't happen often—a person voluntarily calling to come out and list a home. One of our new salespeople had just received an incoming call from a woman anxious to sell her property. We had recently sold a home on the same street. Our "sold" sign broadcast we were the people to contact if a seller wanted action.

The salesperson was both happy and nervous. Somewhat intimidated he asked for my help in placing the property on the market.

I offered to come out with him and help. My ego was at work. If I had known then what I know now, I would have handled the situation differently. Today, I would have sat down and counseled him, role-played with him what the seller's objections might be. Then I would suggest he complete the presentation independently and if he failed, I'd make the second effort and accompany him on a subsequent trip.

We drove together in his car. After bonding with the seller, we all sat down in the living room to discuss price and reason for selling. By our questions, we knew she was ready to move. I looked at the new salesperson and said, "Well, get your briefcase and let's write out some details on an agreement."

A startled look flashed across his face and he whispered, "I don't have my briefcase with me."

I said, "Well, go to the car and get it."

"It's back at the office." At first I was extremely uptight, but I kept it inside.

Upon reflection, I wondered how I could be angry with him. He was the student; I was the teacher. Why hadn't I double-checked to see if he was prepared? Besides, I didn't have my briefcase with me. Airline pilots have a checklist at hand to verify what is needed to prepare for a flight. Salespeople could learn a lot by using a similar tool.

Our immediate goal was to get a psychological commitment from the client. We needed something tangible to keep, as I didn't wish to lose the transaction to our competition. I asked if she had any paper in the modest dwelling. After several minutes rummaging in the back room, she emerged with the only writing material in the house—a new paper towel roll.

We wrote out the detailed terms of the transaction twice and initialed the basic understanding subject to her approval of the final contract and provided her with the second copy. Later that day, my salesman returned with a professionally completed copy.

◆　◆　◆　◆　◆

We both learned a valuable lesson. The Boy Scout
motto is "be prepared"—
or at least have a paper towel handy.

MRS. EVEREADY

*"I have a lifetime contract. That means I can't be fired
during the third quarter if we are ahead
and moving the ball."*

—LOU HOLTZ

Mrs. Eveready was one of my first real estate customers. A number of years previously, I had sold her a two-bedroom home and now she was in the market for a larger one. She described her needs in great detail. The home had to be in the city of Bellflower, the northern part of town, preferably near the high school. She needed a three-bedroom, two-bath home with a den and a double–attached garage. It also had to have a swimming pool.

I searched high and low. The sales force was alerted to be on the lookout. Mrs. Eveready helped. Every time she read an advertisement about a place that generally resembled what she wanted, I received a call. In scanning the classifieds, she became Sherlock Holmes. One of our salespeople finally had the answer—a listing with the exact requirements. I immediately contacted her. My enthusiasm knew no bounds.

"Mrs. Eveready," I exclaimed, "I've found the answer for you." There was a momentary silence and then Mrs. Eveready explained that she had been about to give me a call. "I wanted to tell you what we have done," she said. I spoke to myself, "Mrs. Eveready, what on earth have you done?"

Two days prior to my phone call, Mrs. Eveready had been invited to a Sunday barbecue with some friends in the adjacent city of Norwalk. During the late morning, a young man had knocked on the door. He was holding an "open house" across the street. He invited Mrs. Eveready's friends and their guests to come preview the home. They all agreed to go.

The home had four bedrooms, not three, but it was well laid out. Having one bath made it somewhat inconvenient. Nevertheless, the children would soon be grown and gone. The single, detached garage could not hold both cars; however, it would be a reasonable compromise to leave the old Plymouth outside. The home had no pool, but it did have beautiful trees in the backyard. Norwalk was not quite Bellflower but that was offset by the fact they were within walking distance of their friend's home. They made a low offer that they never expected to be accepted—but surprise of surprises—it was.

She went on to thank me for my services and said, "If I ever buy another home, it will certainly be through you." I wished her all the best in her new home. When I hung up, I was frustrated and resentful.

But I had learned a valuable lesson. There are many Mrs. Evereadys in this world. They are mostly decent, honest, and loyal. The validity of our contracts with them depends on the service we provide and the bond we create. I believed Mrs. Eveready really knew what she wanted. But I had not completed my homework or probed enough.

◆ ◆ ◆ ◆ ◆

My mistake was that I had not taken control.
I paid a price for my carelessness.

I ENJOY
A GOOD BET

*"Anybody can win—unless there happens
to be a second entry."*

—GEORGE ADE

I enjoy a good bet with company associates. One bet tested my potential abilities as a butler. My challenger had his full mustache at stake. If he lost, it would be shaved at a company breakfast seminar. If he won, I would be his manservant for a full weekend. He would win those services and spend a skiing weekend at our condo in Mammoth. He was highly motivated not only to retain his mustache but to have the "top banana" at his beck and call. He produced the sales— I lost the bet.

Not only did I serve as his footman, he supplied me with the butler's uniform. My wife was there to appreciate the event. She was particularly helpful explaining to him the "extras" he could request. I made his breakfast, polished his shoes, lit his cigarettes, and even put snow chains on his tires. However, I did refuse to ski down the slopes in the rented butler outfit.

What motivates us to produce such marvelous results? A favorite mustache was the key in this contest. What is the formula needed to press the "hot button" in each of us?

Many people believe that business requires a gregarious personality, a wide circle of personal contacts, and years of experience. Although these factors help, they are by no means the answer to what makes a salesperson successful.

What if I asked a salesperson to go out and make 1,000 cold contact phone calls? You'd probably think—impossible! It would seem overwhelming. What if it was reduced to a tangible reward that compelled results? "I'm going to give you $30 for every call you make, successful or not." The results become very real. Could it now be done in one week? Forty-eight hours? Or by noon tomorrow?

The goal is tangible, the reward evident.

The salesperson winning the butler bet had a short-term goal with a 30-day termination date. He obtained a great reward and would have paid an enormous penalty if he'd not achieved that goal.

It would be ridiculous to suggest this type of strategy is the only way we can or should operate.

♦ ♦ ♦ ♦ ♦

Self-competition and goal setting are inseparable twins. Set yourself some tangible monthly goals, build in a reward if you achieve them, and just as important, sacrifice something (besides the missing commissions) if you don't.

THE SECOND
BATTLE
OF BRITAIN

*"The mass of men lead lives of quiet desperation.
What is called resignation is confirmed desperation."*
—HENRY DAVID THOREAU

In 1942, the British fought for their freedom against the Nazis—
with brave young pilots flying their Spitfires in the famous "Battle of
Britain." For me, a youngster, it was the first battle of Britain. Later
in life I became aware of the second battle.

I watched a documentary on Britain long after World War II. It
featured my hometown, Newcastle-Upon-Tyne. The region's major
industries were shipbuilding and coal mining. A graphic scene featured a helicopter crew's view of a shipyard at 4:45 in the evening,
15 minutes before quitting time. The gates had been locked to keep
in the workers as they crowded around the exit. At 5:00 the whistle
blew, the gates swung open, and the employees made their escape—
a mad dash to do whatever they did when they weren't working.

According to the program, Britain was facing extreme economic
problems as trade unions were all but taking over the country. Private enterprise was under attack. I'd grown up with coal miners and
ship builders. Here were men who hated their jobs so much they
couldn't wait to leave. How futile they must have found their lives
to be. They had not discovered an occupation they enjoyed. If they
had, time would have flown.

As an immigrant in New Zealand in my late teens, I worked two
jobs: salting down cowhides in a tanning factory during the day and
washing dishes in a restaurant at night. Salt holes at my fingertips

due to my daytime work made the hot water intolerable. I was finally fired at the restaurant for using lukewarm water. At first I was devastated. How could anyone not appreciate my efforts? The dishwashing job was quickly replaced with better pay and more appreciation, working for New Zealand Forest Products in a laboratory as an assistant.

◆　◆　◆　◆　◆

Does life at work need to be a drudge?
It requires courage to
change your job and your lifestyle.

PLOWING
THE 40 ACRES

"Time is a storm in which we are all lost."
— WILLIAM CARLOS WILLIAMS

Prospecting is intimidating to most salespeople. We hear about the fearless salesperson who knocks continually on doors or calls constantly on the telephone. The superhuman who does not accept rejection. "Old Ironsides," if such a person really does exist, is a rare phenomenon. Most of us have to mentally gear up to go out and fight the battle. It's tough when the majority of people say "No!" to your worthwhile propositions and offers of service.

Several hundred years ago, there was a pilgrim's farm. The farm tools were primitive. The most backbreaking chore was plowing the land. Pushing that heavy plow behind the horse team created aches and pains. But plowing those 40 acres of ground meant the cycle of life could be sustained. The crop was used to feed the farmer, his young family, and the farm animals. This, in turn, furnished products to sell at market. Prospecting and plowing have a lot in common.

The pilgrim farmer realized it was critical to plow his field. If he let it go any longer, the seeding would be affected by the weather. He had procrastinated for several weeks because plowing was extremely distasteful. On Monday, the beginning of a new week, he made the decision to get out and plow. He reached the barnyard as the sun edged over the horizon. With the team of horses hitched to the plow, he was ready.

Out of the corner of his eye, he noticed the woodpile was low. It required replenishing for the cooking pots and winter warmth to fight off the bitter cold. His ax and saw were close by. He decided to

36

complete the chopping. He worked feverishly until the woodpile was stacked high.

He noticed the fence next to the woodpile needed repair. The last cord had pressed too hard and caused some damage. He decided to fix it. It took longer than expected, but he finally stood back with pride and reviewed his work.

Making his way back to the plowing, he heard Betsy, his favorite cow, bellowing loudly inside the barn. She needed milking, so he grabbed a pail and took care of the chore.

When he finished that, he heard the clucking of chickens in the hen house. Why not pick up the eggs now and get it out of the way? Soon the eggs were gathered in a huge basket.

His journey down to the hen house brought him to the hog pens. It was time to feed the hogs.

Returning to the plow, he noticed the sun sinking in the west. He unhitched the horses and put them back into the barn. Tomorrow, he promised himself! Tomorrow!

No one could deny he had put in a full day's work. He hadn't been lazy. His day had been filled with useful activity. The sad fact was he hadn't accomplished his A priority. The Bs and Cs had been carried out. Why? One could speculate, but I suggest he unconsciously avoided what was most unpleasant and difficult. For him, it was plowing the fields. For a salesman, it could very well be prospecting!

◆　◆　◆　◆　◆

*If we first accept and recognize the real reason we
don't prospect, namely fear of rejection,
then we are on the road to conquering it. Of equal
benefit is to realize the prospect is
not rejecting you, but your product or service.
Learning to separate yourself from your
product or service allows you to survive rejection.*

YOU'LL LIKE
WHAT I DID NEXT

"If television encouraged us to work as much as it encourages us to do everything else, we could better afford to buy more of everything it advertises."
—CULLEN HIGHTOWER

Dick Lott lived his life in a wheelchair. He and his wife, Mary, also a paraplegic, were having a small custom home built by our development company. He had requested an extra wide hallway, ramps at the door entrances, and special fixtures in the bathroom. During the course of construction, we became good friends.

Dick had worked for Los Angeles County for nine years. Fiercely independent, he decided he wanted to be a real estate salesperson. At first, I discouraged him. It would be difficult, at best, for him to place homes on the market and show them. He persisted until we agreed to a compromise.

Dick would still work for the county during the day and would work at real estate evenings and weekends. After enduring this "serving two masters" for four months, he finally left his county employment and devoted all his efforts to selling. Although not a superstar in production, he made a good income.

Like all salespeople, Dick had his highs and lows. In his third year of sales, he found himself in a slump and decided to quit. First, he wanted to talk with me about it, so we decided to go to lunch. He insisted on driving—he had special driving attachments on his car—and also insisted on buying lunch.

By then, I knew Dick was too good to give up on himself and leave the business. He had proven it with his two-year track record.

38

In trying to reach out on the way to the restaurant, I asked questions. I prompted him to tell me about his yesterday. He replied, "Yesterday was a bad day."

I wanted to know why, so I asked, "What time did you get to the office?"

"Eleven o'clock," he replied sheepishly. He normally arrived much earlier. "I had chores to do around the house for Mary—washing dishes and vacuuming." I knew Mary was quite capable of doing this herself but did not pursue his response.

I then asked, "Dick, when you worked for the county, what time did you arrive at work?"

"Eight-thirty," he replied.

"If you had showed up at 11, would you have kept your job?"

"No," he said. "I would have been fired."

"Then why is it any different working for yourself? Have the self-discipline to choose a time each day. Either 8:30 or 9:00, but be consistent." Then I asked, "Upon arrival at 11, what did you do?"

"I wasted an hour."

"How?" I asked.

"I called lenders on a loan they wouldn't make."

With further probing, I learned that Dick had sold a two-bedroom home and flower shop on a single lot. It was dual-use zoning. He was seeking 80 percent financing, which was impossible. Lenders would go a maximum of 70 percent on that type of property. The property had been off the market for 30 days.

Dick had not told either the buyer or seller he was unable to obtain the loan. It was eating away at him to the point that he couldn't function. We agreed that he would re-interview the seller and have him agree to carry a second trust deed for 10 percent of the sales price.

Dick told me then that he had taken an hour-and-a-half lunch. Normally it takes us half that time to eat, so I was curious why he had been gone so long. Had he been with a customer? No, he had been with another salesperson discussing their bowling league. They hadn't been doing well and needed a new strategy. I told him he'd wasted three hours of time—his 90 minutes plus the other agent's 90.

"You'll like what I did next," Dick blurted out. He'd caught onto where I was taking our conversation. "I read two chapters in a book on motivation." I told him the idea was great but the timing wrong. "Dick, the time to read is either early in the morning or late at night. Not during your golden hours of production."

I asked, "What did you do next?"

"I spent one-and-a-half hours calling around a new property I'd just put up for sale."

I asked what time he'd gone home.

"Five o'clock."

"What time was dinner?"

"Six."

"Did you have any evening appointments?"

"No."

"What time did you go to bed?"

"Ten."

"What did you do between 6 and 10?"

"Watched television."

If I had casually asked Dick how many hours he had worked the previous day, he would have said six. In effect, he had worked one-and-a-half dollar-productive hours.

Dick accepted some tough criticism. Before our conversation, he believed he had worked a full day. I suggested he use his daily planner and record for a one-week period exactly what he was accomplishing in one five-minute interval. He agreed; he really didn't want to quit. Not too long after, he got back on track and was doing extremely well.

By the way, how was your yesterday?

◆   ◆   ◆   ◆   ◆

Constantly ask yourself the question,
at this moment, is what I'm doing the highest
and best use of my time?
Should I do it, delegate it, or ditch it?

YOU HAVE THE POTENTIAL OF BEING A FINE SPEAKER

*"It usually takes more than three weeks to prepare
a good impromptu speech."*
—MARK TWAIN

The average person fears making a public speech more than dying. In 1967 I gave my first short speech at a Realtor Private Property Week meeting. With 300 people in the audience, I wanted to do my best announcing the keynote speaker. My previous public-speaking experience had been talks in front of a small captive audience—my sales staff of 10. It had not occurred to me that I would be petrified in front of a large group.

With 300 pairs of staring eyes, I had never felt so self-conscious. The sweat formed on my brow. When I stood up, my mind sat down. My knees felt weak. Without the aid of the lectern, I would have collapsed on the spot.

Stuttering a few words, I tried to communicate how much the speaker would captivate the audience. After an eternity, I stumbled off the platform and vowed I would never put myself through that agony again.

Larry Moshier came to my rescue. A mild-mannered, gray-haired fatherly type in his mid-70s, he was the editor of a local newspaper. He asked how I had felt. "Bloody terrible," I replied. He offered that in spite of my feelings of inadequacy, I had the potential of becoming a fine speaker.

"But," he added, "you certainly need a lot of help." Larry suggested I join him at his Toastmasters Club the following Monday

41

morning for breakfast. Attending this self-improvement organization every week for the following five fruitful years, I learned the skill through self-analysis and constructive criticism by fellow members.

People needn't be concerned about public speaking. Each of us has unique experiences, providing us with material that could be of interest to others. There is no reason we shouldn't take this material and turn it to our advantage. The group might be a few people at a staff meeting or a huge crowd filling an auditorium. In addition, how you prepare could mean success at a planning commission meeting or persuading a group of investors to go along with your project.

If asked to speak, it's because people have the confidence that you can pass on what you know about a topic. Who will be in your audience? Why are they going to be there? What interests them? What do they need to know?

- Sweat while preparing. You'll sweat less once in front of the audience. Research your subject thoroughly. Check out books at a library. Collect timely magazines and newspaper articles. Research the Internet. Talk to an expert on the subject and pick his or her brain. This will help round out your speech. Your goal is to learn more than you'll ever use. It will give you the confidence to inspire you and your audience.

- Organize and begin writing. A good speech consists of three separate parts: the introduction, the body, and the summary. Create an upbeat impact in the beginning. The audience will make up its mind very quickly. Break the ice by telling a story about yourself in which you may have failed. Self-deprecating humor always works. Audience members can identify with similar events. One of my favorite lines is, "The emcee makes me sound so ancient— as a matter of fact, my wife tells me I'm so old my blood type is now extinct."

Jokes at the opening are fine, provided they make a point that ties in with the topic. Don't tell dirty jokes. They always fail with a percentage of the audience.

The four objectives in the main body of the speech deal with: (1) entertainment, (2) instruction, (3) the credibility to persuade, and (4) the ability to inspire. With research you can blend all four.

The summation is the closing. It's asking for the order. Give your audience a hint that you are coming to the end. Such words as, "in closing," or "I have one last thing to say," or "finally." But be sure you eventually stop talking!

- Use 3 x 5 index cards to arrange thoughts. Use them to rehearse and rearrange to fit the speech. The key is to deliver your speech as if you're not reading it.

  Make it appear to be spontaneous even if you have scripted every word. Talk to yourself in a mirror. Communicate point-by-point rather than word-for-word. It takes several weeks to prepare a good spontaneous speech.

- Most good talks are between 30 and 40 minutes. When instruction is for a three-hour period, have at least one break. Take advantage of audience participation. Use role-play workshop activities. Make sure they are physically involved in the subject matter.

- Eye contact is extremely important. Pick out three or four members of the audience in different parts of the room. Choose people who look positive and pleasant. The rest of the audience will fall in line.

  The larger the crowd, the easier it is for you to reach them. Any positive response is multiplied and amplified. There is more opportunity for a positive response than negative, because audiences are sympathetic toward a speaker.

- Don't be afraid of the butterflies. If you are tense, it's all right. A little stage fright pumps the adrenaline. Forget about yourself—focus on your audience. You'll do just fine.

◆ ◆ ◆ ◆ ◆

Learn to speak in front of an audience. If this can be accomplished, then subsequent "one-on-one" communication can become extremely effective.

YOU HAVE AN INSURMOUNTABLE IMPEDIMENT

"Wisdom is the reward you get for a lifetime of listening when you'd have preferred to talk."

—DOUG LARSON

President Kennedy had a goal to reach the moon. What he didn't foresee was once there, most of the aerospace engineers were going to be laid off. George was one. He became a realtor.

George had a high IQ but an extremely low AQ (awareness quotient). He was not a people person. George loved to talk, but dialogue never seemed to work for him.

One day I was walking by a conference room and overheard a conversation between George and his customers, a young couple wanting to buy their first home. George was investigating their credit application, which revealed a minor credit problem. He said, "You people"—he didn't call them John and Mary, although he'd been with them for several hours— "have an insurmountable impediment." The young couple wondered what kind of strange disease they had just contracted.

George never sold that piece of property and never understood why. He was talking at the customers—not with them. There was no bonding—no relationship.

◆　◆　◆　◆　◆

You can't sell any product to any customer unless you sell yourself first.

THAT'S ONE SMALL STEP FOR MAN, ONE GIANT LEAP FOR MANKIND

*"Success generally depends upon knowing
how long it takes to succeed."*
—CHARLES, BARON DE MONTESQUIEU

The year was 1951. I was attending a commercial boys' school in Newcastle-Upon-Tyne, England. One of my favorite classes was general science, because the chemistry bottles, Bunsen burners, and continual experiments were fascinating. On the back of the classroom wall was a bulletin board upon which the science teacher pinned articles of interest. An eminent author had just written a piece for the *London Times* on why it would be impossible for man to reach the moon. Although I cannot recall the details, he documented "facts" on why a combination of elements would be the undoing of anyone foolhardy enough to risk such a journey. Since I was young and impressionable, I was totally convinced his arguments were sound.

In 1960, President Kennedy set a goal to reach the moon within ten years. Nine years later an astronaut stood on the moon.

In the late 1960s back in England on vacation with my wife and children, we were staying at the Red Lion Inn in Carlisle. We visited the TV lounge, which was crowded with people. Across the street stood a castle built a thousand years earlier by the Norman conquerors, yet everyone's attention was focused on the flickering TV screen. Neil Armstrong was taking his first step on the moon's surface. It brought back strong memories of my science class days and the journalist's erroneous information in his short essay. The castle across the street was juxtaposed against the TV showing us, "One small step for man!" What a vivid demonstration of 1,000 years of progress.

◆ ◆ ◆ ◆ ◆

Your goals are reachable, too,
if you believe in yourself and make
the commitment to them.

JOSKO PULLED OUT A LITTLE RED BOOK

"Advice is sometimes transmitted more successfully through a joke than grave teaching."

—BALTASAR GRACIAN

My wife has a cousin named Josko who is a judge in Croatia, which used to be part of Yugoslavia. When we visited Josko in the early 1970s, Marshal Tito was still alive and governed Yugoslavia with an iron fist. We discovered, however, that Yugoslavia was the most capitalistic communist country in the world, with a lot of private enterprise.

We visited a lovely city called Mostar; it boasted a beautiful old bridge built 400 years ago. Unfortunately, it has since been bombed by the warring factions in the recent Bosnia conflict.

We were having lunch with Josko in a restaurant built into a cave. The outside temperature was 90 degrees; inside it was a comfortable 70 degrees.

After finishing our meal, Josko and I relaxed and talked. He did not speak a great deal of English and I didn't speak any Serbo-Croatian, but somehow we were able to communicate. Josko pulled out a little red book that was actually a payment book. He proudly showed me he was paying monthly dues to the Communist party and he took the occasion to brag that I had no such book in the United States. Furthermore, we in America were unfortunate not to belong to such a fine political system.

I smiled and wondered how to respond. How could I advise him on the benefits of capitalism over communism without offending

47

him? With a flash of inspiration, I pulled out my American Express card and said, "No, I don't have a Communist card, but you should try one of these. I assure you, it will get me quite a bit further than yours."

◆   ◆   ◆   ◆   ◆

Use a visual prop whenever one is available to reinforce your position. It could be a yellow pad, a progressive revelation of a page of notes, or a credit card.

HOME IS A VERY POTENT FORCE

*"You have not converted a man because
you have silenced him."*

—JOHN MORLEY

There were tears in the eyes of Matt, my father-in-law, as he stood on the deck approaching the small harbor on the island of Vis in Yugoslavia, the place where he was born. It was an emotional trip for him that had been greatly anticipated.

We had left the Dalmatian coast, traveling on a small vessel similar to those that sail to Catalina Island in Los Angeles County. This little island, located out in the middle of the Adriatic Sea, was once covered with emerald-green vineyards. Now, the vineyards had vanished, returned to acres of gray barren rocks. The contrast was shocking to him.

It was 1970. Matt's last visit had been 40 years earlier, when he was just 30 years old. What he had left behind was lost forever. There were tears in his eyes. It's wrenching when we leave our places of birth and return years later and confront dramatic changes. Everything seems much smaller and nothing seems quite as beautiful as remembered.

The population on Vis had greatly decreased since Matt had gone. Most of the young people had left the island to seek their educations and fortunes elsewhere. Matt had done the same. In the early 1920s, he arrived in San Pedro, California, as an immigrant. After marrying, he built his first home there in 1934 for $3,300.

My wife Tomazina and I, our children Elaine and Kirk—youngsters at the time—and Tomazina's parents, Helen and Matt, were spending three weeks in Yugoslavia.

We flew to Rome, spent a day, and then caught a flight to Dubrovnik. This beautiful city was considered one of the best-preserved medieval walled cities in the world. Tomazina had relatives living within the walled area. It was a delight—almost a mystical experience—to walk around. The city walls jutted out from the coastline. Sadly, Dubrovnik was badly damaged by the warring factions during the conflicts in the former Yugoslavia.

Following that visit, we took a steamboat up the Adriatic through the Dalmatian Islands. It was stormy, but I was the only member of the family to get seasick. Everyone else seemed to handle the voyage. When we arrived at the dockside harbor in Split, Matt's family was there to welcome us. At first he didn't recognize his brothers and nephews. But they soon were reacquainted and there were hugs and kisses all around.

Matt's brother, Tony, had been a partisan during World War II, fighting with Tito against the Nazis. He mesmerized us with stories of some of his harrowing experiences. Part of our trip was a DC3 flight to Zagreb and Tony accompanied us. It was interesting to watch as brave a man as he nervously climb into an airplane for the first time in his life.

Yugoslavia is a beautiful country and the islands off the coast are particularly spectacular—scenically beautiful and still rich in cultural tradition. One of the small islands we visited, called Bisovo, was the island where Matt's family still held some land. A few members of the family still tended crops as they had done for decades. There were only eight people on the island and the only "traffic" was two donkeys.

We made our way up the rocky trail to the hilltop that overlooked hundreds of miles of open ocean. We reached the small community and found that the village chapel had lightning damage over its entrance. It and the schoolhouse were in disrepair and abandoned. Mulberry, wild cherry, and fig trees laded with fruit dotted the landscape.

Further along, we found a row of dwellings. Most were abandoned, but one elderly woman still lived there and came running toward us with a joyous welcome. She was dressed in peasant clothing, with a babushka around her graying hair and a patched apron covering her ankle-length house dress. We'd arrived at the family home. It was such a nostalgic experience to walk through the house, trying to imagine what life would have been like when the family occupied it. On the second floor, wide open to the world, we discovered a rough homemade bed that still held a tattered straw mattress. This was where Matt's mother had given birth to him. I was recently reminded of the power our roots have over us and the importance we place on the homes we occupy when I read headlines blaring out of *The Los Angeles Times* on August 8, 1995:

House in Ruins, Still Home for Returnee

Petrinja, Croatia—The wait to return home for Borislav Belsic lasted almost four years. In that time he lost an eye and most of a leg. When he reached his doorstep, he barely found a roof overhead. But Belsic and a handful of other Croats trickling into this newly recaptured town were not complaining. They were home after all, something they could only dream about just a few days ago. " Would have killed myself if they didn't let me come."

◆   ◆   ◆   ◆   ◆

There is an obsession about having a place we call our own. There is a compelling need to own our own home. What it does to us psychologically! What price we're prepared to pay to keep it! Even when tyranny has stolen our voice. What tremendous losses we suffer when the privilege is taken away from us! Home ownership is a very potent force. It's also a great reminder of the freedoms we enjoy in the United States. I have used this experience on a number of occasions to illustrate to a prospective buyer the power of home ownership.

KEROSENE LAMPS "SHED LIGHT ON THE OCCASION"

*"We Athenians hold that it is not poverty
that is disgraceful, but the failure to
struggle against it."*

—PERICLES

Harrison Ford's movie *Witness* dealt with a Philadelphia detective forced to hide in an Amish religious community in Pennsylvania.

The story brought back memories of a sales conference trip in 1976 when I toured Indiana with the president of its state real estate association. We traveled from city to city each day to address realtor audiences.

Honored to have been asked to speak at Notre Dame University in South Bend, we were accompanied by local reporters who took pictures of our group on the morning of the talk. They lined us up next to a cannon commemorating the American Revolution and asked me to pull the cannon's chain and pose for photographs. Much to everyone's surprise, the cannon went off with a huge blank charge. A deafening noise had windows rattling and people running toward us.

I raised grins and eyebrows remarking, "It's interesting to me that 200 years after the revolution you would have an Englishman fire the Bicentennial cannon. It looks like we've returned."

The Indiana Association president was Dean Kruse, a senator who was very popular with the Amish in Indiana. Kruse had helped keep their schools open, fighting Indiana legislation that threatened

52

them. He asked if I would like to meet one of his Amish friends, a local leader and blacksmith. Accepting the invitation, we had dinner in their home.

Watching the blacksmith trade a repaired wagon wheel for some buckets of paint, I experienced the barter system in action since this religious group rarely used money. There was no electricity, therefore no radio, TV, telephone, refrigerator, or any other modern conveniences in the home. The women sat silently and separated during this social occasion. The food at the dining table was homemade—plain and simple, but nutritious. Kerosene lamps shed light on the occasion and the children spent part of the evening staring in wonderment at Dean's digital watch.

Being inquisitive, I inquired how these wholesome folks spent their lives. Embodying a work-ethic philosophy, living in a farming community, toiling from dawn to dusk, accepting and understanding the basic priorities of life, they skillfully used the kinds of tools proven for hundreds of years. The larger American population could claim that the Amish were living in needless poverty—not recognizing the benefits.

In clothing and shelter, they had no pretensions. They wore simple, practical coverings—even buttons were considered ostentatious. Social activities were governed by a sincere desire to help their neighbors. Self-actualization came through their spiritual activities and devout religious beliefs. What stood out was the effective, efficient order in their lives.

They were oblivious to the temptations that could wrest them away from their goals.

◆　◆　◆　◆　◆

If we, on the outside, could maintain the discipline
of the Amish, how easy it would be to
have the balance of our lives fall into place.

WHERE ARE YOU CALLING FROM?

"Success seems to be largely a matter of
hanging on after others have let go."

—WILLIAM FEATHER

"Reach out, reach out and touch someone." That's an old but familiar tune. The telephone company has excellent marketing on the use of this marvelous instrument.

Traveling down the coast of South Africa as an 18-year-old, I sailed into Capetown. There I met my father's brother, Bob, as the ship docked. He had lived as a stonemason in Johannesburg for many years. He recognized me because I had prearranged to wear a gray suit with a bright red tie.

In subsequent years, I wrote him letters, but there were never any replies. Twenty years later I finally received a letter from him. He had written first to my father. The letter had been returned marked, "Address Unknown." (My father had died during this 20-year period.) He then visited the American Consulate and obtained my address.

Uncle Bob's letter was a pleasant surprise. It also brought a twinge of sadness because he was not aware my father had passed away.

My father's other brother, Jimmy, was alive and well, living in Los Angeles. Uncle Bob and Jimmy were both in their mid-70s. They had not met, talked, or communicated for 32 years.

Uncle Jimmy was unaware that I had received the correspondence. Calling South Africa, I obtained Uncle Bob's telephone number. Ten hours ahead of California time, I put my plan into effect the following Friday morning at 7:00 A.M. Uncle Jimmy, then our company security guard, was asked to come in and sit at my desk. We called him the Captain of the Tower. I picked up the telephone requesting an overseas operator, giving her the phone number without telling Uncle Jimmy who I was calling.

It was 5:00 P.M. Friday in South Africa. If Uncle Bob was going to be home, it should be at this time. The phone rang twice, then picked up. My throat felt constricted. A faint Scottish voice came over the cable, "Hello."

I answered, "Hello, it's Bruce. You wrote a couple of weeks ago."

There was a catch in his voice as he croaked out, "Nephew Bruce?" Then silence. He finally whispered, "Where are you calling from?"

"Los Angeles, California. Hold on, I want you to speak to someone." Reaching over I said, "Uncle Jimmy, I have Uncle Bob on the telephone. Would you like to speak to him?" Tears welled up in his eyes.

They were on the telephone for an eternity—thirty-two years is a long time between conversations. Many family events had taken place. Children had grown, those children had children. Some brothers and sisters had died. It was both a happy and sad occasion. How much had been lost over many years because no one had made the effort to maintain contact!

What a lesson this carried to me. Why do we lose touch with people who mean so much? If we are not prepared to make an effort with people we love, how can we ever be successful in our less personal relationships?

◆ ◆ ◆ ◆ ◆

A business relationship is just that: a relationship.
The thank-you note, the small gift,
the special occasion card, the phone call. They all
add up. Make a special effort to keep in
touch. Reach out, reach out and touch someone.

WHAT HAD I LEARNED TO THIS POINT?

"The greatest mistake is to imagine that we never err."
—THOMAS CARLYLE

As a salesperson, my life has been filled with transactions. The challenge is to determine exactly what the parties want from the negotiating process. My skill helps me understand that process. It's a game of mental gymnastics. Success comes when what appeared to be a painful process is finished as a pleasant, decision-making event occurring in a spirit of cooperation.

Going into a transaction, I assume I'm going to make a deal. Being optimistic, I don't begin with the idea I'm going to fail. By creating a spirit of cooperation, I want the other person to feel I'm forthright, cheerful, confident, and determined to reach a fair agreement.

When you've learned the skills of negotiation, you arrive at acceptable conclusions.

Beginning in management, I was more inclined to be a star than a star builder, wanting as the mentor to show the salesperson how to do it, but mistakenly doing it on his behalf. It took a great deal more patience to allow the salesperson to do it less skillfully than I. After all, I knew how to do it correctly! I sat there and gritted my teeth wanting to jump in, but by not jumping in, allowing him to succeed or fail. If he failed, then I could step in and hopefully save the transaction. By changing, did we lose a few transactions because of that method? Yes, but in the long run, it taught the salesperson how to fish. In catching a fish for him, it would feed him for the day, but leave him hungry the next. By teaching him how to fish, it allowed him to feed himself for a lifetime.

A prospect will always react more favorably when not threatened. Treat prospects with respect, particularly in verbal communication. This is one of the most important negotiating tools. Pay attention not only to the words the customer speaks, but the music behind those words.

The best example of hearing this music came from a long-time friend, Howard Brinton, who's a national real estate trainer. One Sunday Howard called on an old high school buddy to play a game of golf. When his friend took the call, he was in the kitchen with his wife. She was preparing an early dinner for her parents. The husband placed his hand over the receiver and said, "Howard's in town for one day. He wants to play a round of golf. Okay?" His wife protested, "But my parents are coming over for dinner this afternoon." The husband hung in, and responded with, "But it's Howard, my best friend." She then replied, "Then go ahead and enjoy yourselves." But with her tone of voice, the music was, "If you don't stay for dinner, the locks on the doors will be changed."

Selling is never a simple process of convincing someone to purchase. It's the art of creating conditions or an environment that allows the customer to buy and you not to sell. The skill of the salesperson is to put a prospect into a position where he thinks it was his decision to buy.

Testimonials from satisfied customers are critical, too. It's a skill to use the testimonials properly. Nothing is more convincing to a prospect than the hard evidence that others did the same thing you're asking him to do.

A major step forward for a novice salesperson is to realize he does know he doesn't know but is prepared to embrace rejection to discover the path to success, which requires not only seeing the prospect, but persuading the prospect that your product or service fulfills a need. He knocks on doors, he hands out business cards, yet most people never call him. It's far from easy. His self-esteem gets knocked for a loop and he arrives at a point where he's not sure any of his confidence remains. His feelings of insecurity can be intense. He feels rejection acutely. He doesn't feel loved. It's not unlike Willy Lohman in *Death of a Salesman*.

It's a universal experience. Many books have been written about why salespeople fail. Rejection can be a killer, but it needn't be if a salesperson accepts there will be a certain amount of resistance present before the sales pitch even begins. So goes the tale of a salesperson once so down on his lack of success that he decided to quit. But he wouldn't quit until he made a sale. He wanted to go out a winner. Then the sale came and he wouldn't quit for the world. With renewed enthusiasm, optimism, and a new outlook on life, he continued the journey.

It's tough to be looked upon as a manipulator. No one really knows for certain whether the salesperson is actually a friend, whether the love is real or a calculated ploy to take something from them. That's the unfortunate position a salesperson's in. Is he or she for real? If you really do have a need to be of service to people, it eventually shows through. As the saying goes, "You can fool all of the people some of the time, and some of the people all of the time, but you can't fool all the people all the time."

What about the closing? It's not one magic minute but a series of small steps.

◆　◆　◆　◆　◆

Closing tests the highest pressure point for anybody.
Closing, then, is not a moment;
the salesperson who lets it become one is not
a skillful negotiator.

MY FRIEND KARL

*"Experience increases our wisdom but
doesn't reduce our follies."*
—JOSH BILLINGS

Karl Kaiser was an immigrant from East Germany. We met in 1960 when I was knocking on doors in the city of Bell Gardens. He lived in a modest apartment with his wife Christa and their newborn daughter. He came to the door with her cradled in his arms and a huge, toothy smile—his trademark. Newly employed in a manufacturing plant, he was struggling with both his English and finances. Ambitious, enthusiastic, and creative, he was destined to be self-employed.

In the beginning he gave more to our friendship than I. Saving their money, Karl and Christa opened a small factory, which grew and grew. Karl's background was engineering; he was extremely inventive. His specialty became scuba equipment. On the cutting edge with new design regulators, masks, fins, and so forth, he had patents on many of his products.

Our families vacationed together but Karl was the one to go out of his way. We skied together and he also captained a large motorboat. Trips to Catalina and Mexico were not uncommon.

His frustration with our lopsided friendship had finally manifested. One day while we were lunching together I continually looked at my watch. Not that I was bored, I was simply on a time schedule—actually a treadmill—growing my business. He told me that next time I came to lunch not to wear my watch or he'd walk out. Well, I forgot his request and wore my watch the next time we had lunch. He agreed to stay if I turned my watch inside-out on my wrist.

59

Karl died of lung cancer several years later. I had the opportunity to redeem myself somewhat when he was sick, visiting him in his home on several occasions—without my watch—to cheer him up and let him know I really did care.

Recently, I had a conversation with his widow. It has been 16 years since he died and Christa has found another top-notch husband to share her life. She informed me Karl had not been fooled by my wristwatch turning. He had told her that I still looked at my watch, thinking I was fooling him.

So what's my point? I had a better friend than I ever realized. Apparently he accepted me for who I was—forgiving my shortcomings and lack of consideration for his feelings. I hope toward the end I made up for some of my thoughtlessness.

◆ ◆ ◆ ◆ ◆

It requires a constant perception to detect the needs
of others and have an awareness of
what turns them on and turns them off.

SOMETIME NEXT YEAR

"The only joy in the world is to begin."
—CESARE PAVESE

The busy flight pattern corridors into O'Hare airport were jammed because of a snowstorm and we circled our destination with all the other delayed flights. It took us eight hours to fly from Chicago to L.A.—twice the norm.

Twenty-eight-year-old Carl was seated next to me. He and I enjoyed a few cocktails and conversation as the hours passed. He was returning home from Los Angeles where his company had sent him to repair an expensive mainframe computer. Extremely well trained in his specialty, he was earning an excellent income but was frustrated and bitter about one aspect of his occupation.

He made a remark that has remained with me to this day. His company sales representative had sold the computer to the L.A. firm and was earning four times as much as Carl, even though Carl knew more about the machine than the salesperson would ever know. He told me that he'd decided to change careers and go into sales. I agreed. It seemed like a wise decision and asked when he intended to do it. His response was, "Sometime next year." When he said "sometime," I knew that meant "never" and told him. A specific target date needed to be made to achieve the goal; otherwise, he would be repairing computers for the rest of his working life.

Carl was silent a while and I wondered if I'd offended him. If that were the case, he never expressed it. When we finally touched down, he smiled and said that he was going to take me up on my advice.

◆ ◆ ◆ ◆ ◆

It has been said, "Analysis leads to paralysis." We will never have all the answers to all the questions—fear of the unknown prevents many of the commitments we make but never complete. Making those commitments requires specific follow-up and target dates.

THE JIGSAW PUZZLE

"Every man's got to figure to get beat sometime."
—JOE LOUIS

It was November 1974. We were at a real estate office opening.

One of our young agents approached and said, "Bruce, I'd like you to buy me a Lincoln Continental."

Always being hit up for something, I smiled back. "What makes you think I should buy you a car?"

He replied, "Because I'm going to produce more sales than anyone else in the company this December."

We had several hundred salespeople and this agent had never been number 1. A Continental back then cost about $7,000. Mental calculations verified that if he had 15 sales for the month, I would break even. "All right, if you can sell 15, I'll buy you a new Lincoln. If you don't, then you're going to take my wife and me out for the most expensive dinner in Los Angeles."

On the final day of November, I received one of our cardboard sold signs. On the back the agent had outlined a Continental in 15 blank jigsaw puzzle pieces. Using a magazine photo of the car was his device to put me on notice. He said, "I'm going to send you down pieces of my car in glorious technicolor."

He requested I put the cardboard sign on my office wall to look at daily. Five days into the contest I received three pieces of the jigsaw puzzle.

I figured out where the shapes should go, and my three pieces were glued to the sold sign. I then received two more pieces. Seven days into the month he already had five sales. December normally is a slow month because of the holidays.

His sales slowed for a few days. On a visit to our accounting department, I requested a check for $7,000—the price of the car. The check was couriered to the agent unsigned, with a little note: "Dale, I wanted you to see what $7,000 looked like to buy the Continental." Within two days, I got two more puzzle pieces back; he was now at seven. By the 20th, he had made nine sales. I made arrangements for my secretary to visit the Princess Louise, a beautiful ship restaurant docked at the harbor in San Pedro.

Their menus carried colored photos of their meals. She brought back a menu and I circled with a red marker pen "Surf and Turf."

The menu was delivered to him. It read, "Dale: This is what my wife and I are going to enjoy at your expense. Am I looking forward to it!" Within two days, I received two more pieces. At the end of December, he also put five homes on the market for sale. Dale had never produced more than four sales in a single month and now he was setting an almost unbelievable record.

He lost the bet, but did he really lose? He gained so much. What was his motivation?

◆　◆　◆　◆　◆

He found something he really wanted and wanted it
so badly that he pulled out all the stops to
get it. His income could have bought him two
Continentals that month.

IT TOOK ONE PHONE CALL

"It is easy to be brave from a safe distance."

—AESOP

Roy needed to borrow my new Mercedes. He normally drove a beat-up old Chevrolet, but he was on the threshold of making his largest sale. In the real estate business for a few short months, he'd earned only two commission checks. In the 1970s, the average sale in our office was between $25,000 and $30,000.

One day, Roy adoringly watched a former Miss America. She was Tawny Little, a news anchor on one of the Los Angeles stations. She mentioned she was contemplating buying a home in Beverly Hills. Roy wondered if he could sell her that home. Did he have the guts to contact her?

Coming into the office, he lost the courage to call but kept wrestling with the idea all day long until finally, at 3:00 P.M., he made a call to the station and asked to speak with her. Ms. Little's producer came to the phone and said, "I'm sorry, she's busy right now. I'll have her call you back." Roy hung up, believing that he'd been rejected. However, at 5:00 that day, his phone rang. It was Tawny Little returning his call.

Nervously stumbling through each word, he finally said, "Ms. Little, I saw your program on television this morning. Apparently you're interested in buying a home. I'd love to find one for you. Would you mind if I made an appointment?"

"No, I wouldn't mind," she replied. Perhaps she was flattered in having an ardent fan like Roy.

Roy didn't know much about Beverly Hills, but he was prepared to learn. Upon obtaining my instructions, he took my car to Beverly Hills and some Realtor friends researched properties that might be suitable for Ms. Little.

The following weekend, he made arrangements to meet her and again, I was stuck with the antique Chevy.

Roy sold Ms. Little a home in excess of a half million dollars. When he asked her how many other salespeople called her that day wanting to find her a home, her reply was surprising and short: "None." Yet, tens of thousands of people watched that show.

◆   ◆   ◆   ◆   ◆

We are all victims of self-doubt, but Roy only
needed one phone call to
achieve his objectives, overcome his apprehension,
and assure his success.

THE MAGIC
OF AN ORANGE

*"The first and greatest commandment is,
Don't let them scare you."*

—ELMER DAVIS

I had so many plates in the air, they were bound to come crashing down. In 1980 I was developing building projects in numerous locations: 38 ski condominiums at Heavenly Valley at Tahoe, a 32-unit condominium project in Long Beach, a 16-home planned unit development in La Habra, 50 single-family residences in Arizona, and custom homes in both La Habra Heights and San Clemente. In addition, I had recently completed a 47-unit condominium conversion in Long Beach and was in the process of marketing a 60-unit conversion in Phoenix. Almost overnight, interest rates climbed to 19 percent. The 11 percent takeout financing for buyers was no longer available. Asking buyers to pay 8 percent more per loan was too much to ask. Every project came to a screeching halt.

It was disheartening to watch as all our Tahoe condominium presales canceled. Another major project had used up its interest reserve due to a combination of cost overruns of offsite improvements and increased interest. I was tied to a floating prime rate that changed upward monthly. An investor acquaintance once ruefully commented, "If you want time to pass quickly, just give your promissory note for 90 days."

To stem the flow of red ink, I requested an appointment with my bank officers to renegotiate for additional funds and an extension. Two arrived one morning to discuss the situation. In no mood to change the terms of the contract, their buttoned-down, three-piece, shadowy pinstriped suits were a reflection of their dark buttoned-down personalities. Their purpose was intimidation, mine was not to buckle under. It required looking beyond their exterior trappings.

We sat in my office making no headway to compromise. An old mentor told me once that a salesperson's responsibility was to create an environment that encourages others to do business. It required some innovation, as I had been getting nowhere with the Darth Vader duo.

There was a clear plastic bag filled with those huge delicious thick-skinned oranges in my small office. Grabbing the bag, I placed the bag on the table and marched over to the credenza for a box of tissues. Returning to my somber guests, I asked if they would like an orange. It was difficult not to grin at their puzzled look.

Were they thinking, "What is this guy doing? Here we are to negotiate a deal he needs very badly and all he wants to do is play silly games?" They declined the invitation. I indicated that if they didn't mind, I was going to have one.

Turning the plastic bag upside down, four oranges rolled slowly around the table. One of the smaller ones was carefully chosen and I began peeling it. The smell of oranges is better than coffee.

The sweet aroma of the opened orange permeated the room and was extremely tempting. I took twice as long as I normally would to peel. One banker stood up, took off his jacket, loosened his tie, and reached out for an orange. The other finally loosened his tie and timidly picked up his. The mood changed. Everyone was out of uniform. The masks were off.

We dug in with juice dripping everywhere. How can a banker remain intimidating while he is sucking on a slice of your orange? I brought my negotiations to a fruitful conclusion. I obtained a loan increase, an interest reduction, and a repayment extension.

♦ ♦ ♦ ♦ ♦

Oranges can be a great negotiating tool.

THE CONCORDE

"With regard to excellence, it is not enough to know, but we must try to have and use it."

—ARISTOTLE

Flying on the Concorde had always been one of my written goals. The airfare was 20 percent higher than first-class fare on a regular plane. Was it going to be worth it?

My first glimpse of this supersonic, gleaming white bird was as I walked to the boarding lounge. She lay on the runway in the pale English springtime sunlight, poised like a futuristic spaceship with the stars as her destination. There were no lines in the boarding lounge. My boarding pass was embossed in gold and black. Complimentary champagne and tasty appetizers were in plentiful supply. World-renowned newspapers were at my disposal.

The flight was full and departure punctual. The 100 passenger seats were exceptionally comfortable. I saw a scattering of celebrities throughout the cabin as I introduced myself to my neighboring passenger. He was the president of a multinational computer corporation. I wondered about the combined wealth and power of the other passengers.

The flight took three hours and 15 minutes. In a sense, arriving before we left, as there is a five-hour time difference between London and New York. Flying at between 55,000 and 60,000 feet, the sky was a deep purple. From my window, I could marvel at the curvature of a large section of the earth, further enhanced by the glass-encased monitor that protruded from the front cabin bulkhead, which read 1,450 knots—twice the speed of sound. The flight was smooth and the journey across the Atlantic became a relaxed gourmet dinner: sherry and caviar, followed by a choice of shellfish cocktail, several salad options, and a main course of roast beef carved at my seat. Dessert consisted of fresh raspberries and Devonshire cream with cognac topping off the meal.

Reaching my destination, I was whisked through customs—no long, tedious lines. A limousine took me to my connecting Los Angeles flight—and back to the world of reality. Would I do it again? Of course! Would I recommend it to anyone else? You bet! The Concorde over-delivered and under-promised. I experienced more than my expectations.

Although the airplane was a beautiful bird, that in itself is insufficient. This beauty must be matched by service to the traveler. This also holds true for any company or salesperson. Excellence can be reached through the careful execution of the basic fundamentals. Awareness at every stage, making certain that the correct image is portrayed to the customer. The clients' perception of the "overall you" creates either a reservoir of opportunity for future business or destroys any chance for referrals.

◆　◆　◆　◆　◆

Excellence has many faces. Companies
and salespeople who promote excellence have much
in common. You are judged in numerous ways;
the way you greet people, the clothes you wear, the
type of automobile you drive. Do you return
phone calls promptly? Are you there when really
needed? Do they have your respect and
loyalty? All these intricate parts make up the total
you. The brain of a rocket scientist is
not required to recognize these fundamentals. It
demands energy and insight.

BUSSING TABLES

"To some, freedom means the opportunity to do what they want to do; to most it means not to do what they do not want to do."

—ERIC HOFFER

For several years, my wife managed our vacation ownership hotel restaurant and lounge. The hotel normally served a Sunday brunch to 250 customers; however, one Mother's Day there were a total of 657 guests.

There were 500 reservations on the list, but the number swelled with additional walk-ins. Guests began to back up about 11:00 A.M. The kitchen, dining room, and lounge staff responded with a family, teamlike spirit. Although they knew tips would be excellent, enthusiasm went much beyond their financial windfall. But others were needed to pitch in. There was a bottleneck in the system in cleaning off and resetting the tables for new visitors.

My wife suggested I help, and after many years of marriage, I'm well trained and know when not to debate. With the dining room humming, this was a time for discretion. Put in charge of bussing, I cleaned off as many tables as possible. It didn't take long to get caught up in the excitement—the hustle and bustle needed to quickly serve. At first it was difficult to stay ahead, but I soon made progress. A real contest began between the dishwashers and me, since I was determined to stack those trays of dirty dishes. In good spirits, they responded. The whole team was involved. Frantic calls came for water glasses, knives, and forks, creating panicky searches through piled-up crockery, cutlery, and glassware. Finding the proper dish or eating utensil felt like winning a prize.

71

There were a number of overnight guests and local residents who knew us. Comments came thick and fast:

"Tomazina has finally found a job you're qualified to do."

"Hey, busboy, do you have an ashtray?"

"Bruce, take my dessert dish."

Quipping as best I could, I felt like a novice up on skis for the first time.

Suddenly it was 3:00 P.M. and I'd been at it for four hours. Time flies when you're having fun, meeting a lot of fine people, being kidded, and delivering the appropriate response when needed.

Okay, my stint was for a few short hours; I was not tied to a sentence in a dead-end job.

◆   ◆   ◆   ◆   ◆

My belief is there is no possibility of remaining
in such jobs if you give it your all.
Someone will always notice and promote you.
If not, move on—you always have
the freedom of choice. Do your best no matter
what kind of occupation.

OPEN A CAGE
AND A BIRD WILL
FLY AWAY

"Discipline without freedom is tyranny.
Freedom without discipline is chaos."
—CULLEN HIGHTOWER

My mother-in-law Helen was in her late 70s when she suffered a stroke and moved to a rest home. One Sunday I suggested we take her for a drive. It was a prick of conscience since it happened so rarely. My wife offered, "You must have it on your semiannual daily planner." (Why are wives and mothers the most potent engineers of guilt?)

Preoccupied after the visit to Helen and speeding downhill, I hardly noticed an old gentleman sitting on the curb. My wife startled me out of my thoughts, urgently asking me to see if he was in any danger. Pulling up, I noticed one of his shoes was in the road. Casually well dressed, he appeared dazed and breathed in short gasps. Blood dripped from a gash on his forehead and the back of his right hand was scraped; he'd had a bad fall.

I asked if I could help. He looked up but did not respond; there was fear in his eyes. Two days' stubble covered his chin and his false teeth were missing. It made him look even older than his years; I later discovered he was 79. Sitting down, I awkwardly put my arm around his shoulders. We guessed he might be a fellow patient in Helen's rest home. We called them on the car phone, but got a busy signal. We next called 911 giving our location.

"Do you have any identification?" He reached slowly into his pocket and feebly pulled out a large old leather wallet and handed it to me. It was a relief to realize he was alert. Perhaps a previous stroke was preventing him from talking? Apologizing for invading his privacy, I quickly searched his wallet—three times the size of mine. It dawned on me, I was now witnessing his life. His expired driver's license revealed his name and a Torrance address. He'd been well enough in previous years to have it renewed. Next came a doctor's card. We called an answering machine. Then a social worker's card popped up bearing the title Transition Counselor. A person helping in his passage from independence to dependence? Finally, we found a card that read, "In Case of Emergency." It listed a couple in Blythe with a different surname. Maybe a married daughter? A number to call. It rang and rang. There was no answer.

At least two-dozen cards stuffed his wallet listing his former Torrance address. It was as if he were hanging on to his old home. Then came the faded photographs, some 40 to 50 years old. Smiling children, young adults, and a mature lady. His wife? Children, grandchildren?

His breathing was now back to normal. Kleenex stopped the blood flow from his head. We finally connected with the rest home. Recognizing his name, three attendants soon arrived to recover him. He was able to move both legs, stand, and unsteadily climb into the car. A faint smile crossed his lips as we said goodbye. We were angry. Twenty minutes had elapsed and 911 had still not responded. Why had the rest home not been more vigilant? Open a cage and a bird will fly away. He simply wanted his freedom; he craved his independence.

◆　◆　◆　◆　◆

*Do we take our freedom and
independence for granted?*

BE THE BEST
YOU CAN BE

*"Luck is the sense to recognize an opportunity and the
ability to take advantage of it. Everyone has bad
breaks but everyone also has opportunities.
The man who can smile at his breaks
and grab at his chances gets on."*

—SAMUEL GOLDWYN

Over the years, I've taken many airplane trips and met many
people—experiences both good and bad. Traveling to Chicago, I
was on the same flight as my friends Seb Sterpa and his wife, Carol,
who were sitting behind me. We were having a pleasant conversation when a passenger sat down next to me. He introduced himself
as Larry; I told him my name and that was the extent of the conversation.

I asked Seb where he was staying in Chicago. The Continental
Plaza, he answered. In jest I told him that it was a lousy hotel. Why
wasn't he staying at a nice hotel like me—the Drake? I received an
immediate tap on the shoulder from Larry and with a half smile told
me that he totally disagreed.

He then handed me his business card. He was the general manager of the Continental Plaza. Backpedaling, I told him I was only
teasing and agreed that the Continental was a very fine place to stay.

Seb later told me that instead of the ordinary room he'd booked,
he received a suite, complimentary flowers, and champagne. One of
my childhood friends happened to be flying in from England that
weekend. He too had booked at the Continental and received special treatment.

Upon returning to Los Angeles, I received a letter from Larry May. It read, "Bruce, I wonder where you will be staying the next time you're in Chicago? Your friend, Larry."

Where else, I thought. Larry's attitude, humor, and creativity certainly won me over. Out of sheer coincidence, he had maximized the situation and had made believers out of Seb, Carol, my English friend, and most of all me.

◆　◆　◆　◆　◆

Someone once wrote, "In the ordinary business of life, industry can do anything which genius can do, and very many things which it cannot."

DO WE REALLY HAVE TO LISTEN TO ENGLEBERT HUMPERDINCK?

"The whole is greater than the sum of its parts."
—ANONYMOUS

The image we project is a series of little bits and pieces that make up the whole person. We are observed from many angles. It's not my design to take our particular dining experience and blow it out of proportion, but it provides some insights.

We discovered the Jazz Bistro in Puerto Vallarta by accident, flying down to this Mexican seaside resort for a midweek getaway. What attracted us to the Bistro was its unique location adjacent to a bridge and a river. What kept our attention was its beautiful Mediterranean Moorish design—heavy Spanish tile, well-designed wrought iron, bright blue canopies and inviting entry, and a feeling of class and ambiance. The restroom was super clean. We couldn't resist the temptation that evening and took a long taxicab ride from our hotel back to our find, knowing instinctively we'd have a great meal.

The hostess was bright and cheerful, and we were quickly taken to a special table that had a view of the river, cascading from recent rainfall. The owner had paid careful attention to details, from wall coverings to furniture. The dining area was spotless and we felt good about the kitchen we could not see. We ate lobster served by a well-trained waiter, impeccably dressed in a well-chosen uniform. We noticed breadcrumbs swept from the tablecloth, coffee cups atop saucers covered with paper napkins. I asked a question about a jazz singer performing during dinner and the waiter returned with the answer.

The bill was large, but we gladly paid. It was a truly professional establishment, and the employees were serious about their chosen field.

Wanting a view of the city for our next evening's meal, we spotted the Capistrano perched on a hillside overlooking the harbor and beautiful sunsets. Reaching the dining room level required the use of a small outside elevator.

Visiting hotels during the day, we noticed "free coupons" for complimentary drinks at the Capistrano. A negative thought entered my head. Why do they promote business this way? The Bistro had not used this marketing technique. As we arrived, a ten-year-old Mexican charmer was responsible for the elevator. We tipped him but had mixed emotions about having someone so young in charge. It was a small point, so I shrugged it off.

Walking to the entrance of the dining room, we were greeted by the warm and friendly maitre d'. As we joked about my lack of Spanish, I noticed that this large, dark dining room was virtually empty. Would we like to eat outside on the balcony overlooking the city lights? There were no locals—unlike at the Bistro. American and Canadian tourists were having their photographs taken. The seats were uncomfortable and the white paint on the wrought iron chairs had been chipped away. It was a slow evening, with seven waiters serving between 25 and 30 diners. The advertised "live music" did not materialize; instead we heard Englebert Humperdinck on tape. One of the waiters was imitating the songs for the enjoyment of the other waiters who stood around and laughed. The customers didn't have quite the attention the entertaining waiter received. The pork ribs were superb, but the steak was tough. The French onion soup came partially spilled on the plate beneath the bowl. The coffee came the same way—spilled on the saucer.

The waiters were dressed in casual tropical shirts, some unkempt and rumpled. Our waiter had difficulty opening the wine bottle; an older waiter came to his rescue. He also miscalculated the bill and had to do it over. The restaurant demanded an ID when I used my Visa card. Yes, we noticed the little things. The food got mixed reviews and the premises had seen brighter times. Perhaps a future cocktail at sunset would be okay but never another meal.

♦   ♦   ♦   ♦   ♦

We truly are judged on the sum total
of our many parts.

ERADIO

"Luck happens to those who are prepared.
Miracles sometimes occur, but one has
to work terribly hard for them."
—CHAIM WEIZMANN

How do you make your mark? I was teaching a three-day seminar for 150 realtors taking their Certified Residential Broker designation course. I noticed Eradio Diaz in the front row, a blind Cuban refugee who had passed his real estate examination orally.

At the first break, I learned he was managing an office of 20 salespeople. Eradio was there to gain additional management expertise.

Working as a real estate salesperson, his father was his assistant, chauffeuring his son's specially designed limousine. Eradio's typewriter was positioned in the back of the car; he typed contracts by touch, knowing exactly where to place a specific line of information. In addition, he owned a Braille calculator for completing his backup numbers.

When with buyers, they "showed" Eradio property. During the process he asked the buyers to describe each room as they inspected the home together and always requested they let him be aware of the amenities that appealed to them the most. The seller's net sheets and buyer's closing costs were calculated by the prospects participating as Eradio guided them through the process.

Returning to Los Angeles, I called Eradio to receive permission to write his story in the *California Association of Realtors* magazine. His mother answered the phone and said Eradio was not home. She'd explained he'd had a problem with his car and the mechanic was unable to repair it. Eradio traveled to the garage and by touch he'd shown the mechanic there was a short in the electrical circuits. The mechanic then fixed the problem.

◆　◆　◆　◆　◆

I was reminded of the old tale, "I was
saddened and defeated because I had no shoes—
until I met a man who had no feet."
Eradio was an inspiration.

THERE MUST BE
A MISTAKE

"Never use a doctor whose office plants have died."
—ERMA BOMBECK

A letter lay on my desk straight from my HMO. Recently taking my biannual physical, the message concerned me. My cholesterol count was 226. The letter carried a warning.

With my heavy exercise program, there must be a mistake! I ran four miles a day, swam five days a week, and worked out with weights twice a week. My ego at work, I quickly called the doctor's office. Despite my alarm, a nurse assured me that my cholesterol count was only slightly elevated. She advised me to watch my diet.

My diet? I requested another appointment, another blood test. Impossible, an elevated cholesterol count? Then little doubts crept in. Thick, juicy steaks, a weakness for hamburgers, butter, cheese, ice cream, and whole milk—all my favorites. Swiss chocolates, English Kit Kat bars, and American chocolate chip cookies, too.

A sense of urgency overtook me. The new blood test was a week away, why not stack the deck? That old competitive spirit and intensity! Losing my sense of balance about the whole damn thing, how much stress did I create to beat the numbers? All of my favorites were cut out of my diet. Dan Bennett once wrote, "Probably nothing in the world arouses more false hope than the first four hours of a diet." In my case, it was going to be different. I re-tested—the following day a call came.

"Mr. Mulhearn, your cholesterol count has dropped to 205— almost normal. Perhaps there was a mistake? Come back in 90 days and we will retest again."

There had been no mistake. I knew better. I've learned to be more careful.

♦ ♦ ♦ ♦ ♦

Exercise alone is not sufficient. Diet is equally important for good health.

ROY ROGERS

"The man who has no imagination has no wings."
—MUHAMMED ALI

Roy Rogers, the King of the Cowboys, passed on in the late 1990s. Roy and I met in the early 1990s when his grandson was married at the Inn in Silver Lakes. Our family owned the 65-unit hotel, restaurant, and lounge. Weddings were catered in the beautiful garden room and exterior patio adjacent to a 27-hole golf course.

Roy attended in his western clothes. He was not tall in stature but that reminded me you measure a person's size from the neck up. In that regard Roy was a giant.

Roy and Dale decided to settle in Apple Valley, California, in the 1970s. They opened their museum on Highway 18 but moved it to Interstate 15 to give it more tourist exposure en route to Las Vegas. The museum resembled an old wooden western fort built in the far west during the Indian wars, and gave the life history of Roy and Dale's careers with photographs, memorabilia from the different movies they had made, and even the result of a taxidermist's expertise with Roy's favorite horse Trigger.

My generation grew up watching Roy in the movies. Roy never shot a man to death. He always rendered the bad guys harmless with a bullet in the arm or shot the pistol out of their hand. There were other featured "stars"—sidekick Pat Brady, Roy's horse Trigger, Dale Evans' horse Buttermilk, their dog Bullet, and the car Nellie Belle. The family operated out of the Double R Bar Ranch. Roy's trademark was his western shirt, big-buckled belt, bandana, and stitched boots.

As kids we had our cowboy heroes—Roy, Gene Autry, and Hopalong Cassidy. Our movie heroes have images to live up to. Our expectations were that on or off the screen they should always look and act the part until the day they died. Roy did; he was the fellow who always shot straight and someone you felt you could trust and rely upon.

Recently I picked up an old movie and watched him chase the bad guys as he tried to save Christmas for a small frontier town. They were trying to burn a bridge over a gorge while the townsfolk were careening across it with their wagons filled with Christmas trees. Roy had a unique yodel and I read somewhere that Bob Hope took one look at him in a saloon and told the bartender, "Give this kid a straight celery tonic."

◆　◆　◆　◆　◆

Roy Rogers was a role model on and off the screen—perhaps not perfect as from time to time he overfed Trigger with lumps of sugar. What a positive hero for all of us. We need more of them in our lives.

TIM CAN MARINATE FILET MIGNON

"Work and play are words used to describe the same thing under differing conditions."

—MARK TWAIN

My brother Tim can marinate and barbecue a tasty filet mignon. However, it was only recently that I realized this hidden talent. I've sampled his turkey, salmon, and pork—all savory and eagerly devoured. He proclaims it's a lot of effort, but it's really his pleasure. Where did he get the inspiration?

Our mother helped inspire. However, I recall my grandmother cooking family meals on an open wood fire in Scotland in the 1940s. Potato pancakes, soda scones, blackberry pies, and her specialty, rabbit stew. The gigantic metal pots allowed huge portions to be ladled out to many hungry mouths. Cooking under such primitive conditions, she still maintained the stability of the fire and the lack of modern controls were balanced with an eagle eye. Her attention was focused— she knew what was needed each moment.

Grandmother had her recipes and her procedures, but there was also that extra "something." Call it sixth sense, or intuition. She did not scientifically measure salt, pepper, spices, or condiments. She knew the benefits of parsley and onions. Pour here, sprinkle there, and then watch it bubble.

Frequent glances at the cooking food, constantly checking with a sniff or a smell. In goes the wooden spoon for a quick taste, then add that little something needed to suit the palate.

Simmer awhile and spoon again, she doctored until correct. It was never spoiled because of diverted attention.

Finally happy with her creation, off it came. A rabbit stew the best it could be, a joy to the family and a tribute to her talent and intuition. No buttons to press or knobs to turn, nothing automatic.

◆ ◆ ◆ ◆ ◆

Building and running a successful business
is no different. It's a combination of
art and science mixed in with an ingredient
called flexibility.

VARIATIONS OF WHITE, BURGUNDY, AND BROWN AT THE CLASS REUNION

"It is in trifles, and when he is off his guard that
a man best shows his character."

—ARTHUR SCHOPENHAUER

One Saturday evening, my wife and I attended her class reunion. I was decked out in a double-breasted dark blue jacket, pleated trousers, and carefully chosen shirt, tie, and accessories. San Pedro High scheduled these affairs in a combination of summer and winter events every five years.

It was a sentimental evening with young disc jockeys playing old songs like "Charlie Brown" and "Elvira." I hated the music of the 1950s and time hasn't made it better. I think the deejay thought we were born before airplanes flew.

As a spouse—not part of the "in crowd"—I felt left out. Tomazina rushed around hugging and kissing old friends while I had one wary eye open if she lingered too long in any one spot. Finding myself sitting next to an attractive woman, I brought my best social graces to bear. We were both caught in the same situation. Her husband was absent, crazily hugging and kissing, trying to relive or recapture the past. We struck up a conversation that was going extremely well until I reached for my full glass of red wine and knocked it over. The white tablecloth became a two-tone burgundy except around its edges. Fortunately, this was my first glass. I reached quickly and smothered the tablecloth in white napkins.

We laughed, but my newfound friend was now extremely alert. The other guests returned and my wife asked who was responsible for the spill. I took the blame in a manly way. She apologized for me, "He really isn't this clumsy as a general rule." I could have survived without her support.

When coffee was served, my lady friend—clearly willing to take a risk—asked me to pour some for her. The damned coffee refused to flow from the thermal carafe. In desperation, I twisted the lid as I poured. There was a flood resembling a break in a dam. Luckily the coffee was not scalding; my left hand and shirt cuff took the brunt of the pour. The tablecloth was now multicolored with variations of white, burgundy, and brown. My wife asked if I would like to dance. I hastily agreed. Upon our return, the woman I'd talked to so intently had vanished. Not wanting to imagine what she was thinking, I was less pompous at the end of the evening than the beginning.

What did I learn?

◆　◆　◆　◆　◆

Don't take yourself too seriously.

LOST IN CHICAGO WITH A JAMAICAN CABBY

*"Clothe the man. Naked people have little
or no influence on society."*
—ATTRIBUTED TO MARK TWAIN

We asked our cab driver to take us to the Indian Lakes Resort. My wife and I had just landed at O'Hare Airport in Chicago. We were headed for a faculty meeting, a two-day computer simulation exercise. Chicago taxi drivers easily whisk their passengers around downtown, but when we asked our cabby to go in the opposite direction, he looked puzzled until I said the hotel was in the small town of Bloomington. He mumbled what appeared to be acknowledgment and took off.

After driving around for a half hour, we learned he was a recent arrival from Jamaica. When he asked if I had a map, I knew then we were in trouble. It was late and there weren't many places open to ask about our whereabouts. Finding ourselves going through a somewhat shabby area, I spotted a neon light beckoning from a neighborhood bar. The cabby stopped and suggested that I go in and ask how we could get to Bloomington. He was in control of the vehicle—I obeyed.

We had been on mileage-plus upgraded airline tickets, seated in first class, so we'd dressed accordingly. I had on a double-breasted, expensively cut jacket, yellow handkerchief, and Italian silk tie. I removed my coat and tie, unbuttoned my shirt, took off the cuff links and rolled up my sleeves. If we have experience in the business of marketing, hopefully we have the gift of perception, which can be used if we are sensitive to our surroundings. With some misgivings, I walked toward the bar. The parking lot was crowded with beat-up trucks and coupes, and a few strategically placed Harleys. Inside, the place was packed and resembled a scene from the '60s movie Easy Rider featuring Peter Fonda, Jack Nicholson, and Dennis Hopper. Dimly lit and vibrating with heavy rock music, the place was filled with pool tables, beer bottles, bandannas, thick cigarette smoke, and sweaty bodies. Despite my wardrobe adjustment, I was still conspicuous. A pretty, young woman leaned provocatively behind the counter. I made a beeline for her, looked into her eyes, and asked my question. I was lost and needed directions to the hotel in Bloomington. She yelled out, "Does anybody know where Indian Lakes Resort is?"

The whole bar stopped to listen. A burly young man in a tank top and jeans yelled, "Yeah," and rattled off a rapid set of directions. As I quickly scribbled on a piece of paper, the young woman noticed I wasn't getting it all down and came to my rescue. "Ed, go slower for him." Ed was obedient; I was humbled but grateful. He had a friendly face; I thanked him and was on my way.

My instincts as a salesperson told me to adjust my appearance before going into the bar. The change of clothing made me more comfortable and able to adapt somewhat to the situation. Even then, I didn't blend in. What if I'd sat down for a drink? Would that have aroused suspicion and curiosity? "Who is this intruder of our space?" By asking for help, I was immediately accepted, no longer a stranger and posing any threat to anyone's station in life. The folks in the tavern could not have been more attentive to my needs and were eager to be of assistance. It was another lesson in humility for me.

We finally arrived at our destination. There could have been another moral to this story about how a taxicab driver can get skillfully lost and maximize his fare. The cab fare was $57.50, less $1.00 to me for being the navigator. I'd thought that between the cabby and me, I was the bright one!

♦ ♦ ♦ ♦ ♦

A professional salesperson is a chameleon,
adapting to fit each occasion and blending in to
reflect the needs of his customer.

SAN JACINTO

"Be prepared."

—BOY SCOUT MOTTO

Hiking can be a healthy exercise. It can also endanger your life if you're not careful.

I should have known better. It was my first time on this trail hiking to the top of the Palm Springs tram on Mount San Jacinto, an elevation rise of 8,200 feet from the desert floor.

With no map and not fully equipped for more than a day, I had been invited by a longtime friend, Dale Lawrence, who had climbed it on four separate occasions, the last time in 1990. I persuaded two good friends to join us—an experienced hiker, Don Dykstra, and a first-timer, Michael Craig. Mike had recently completed a survival fitness course and felt very capable.

As Dale remembered, he had climbed the 8-mile trail in five and a half hours.

We started as early as possible to give us plenty of time, but Don and Mike didn't double-check their equipment at the trailhead. Dale calculated we'd be back by 1:30 P.M., using the tram to return back in time for us to vote.

Normal daily equipment consisted of a miniature first-aid kit, hat, sunglasses, sunblock, insect repellent, gloves, windbreaker, flashlight, 2 quarts of water, a sandwich, a couple of bananas, some tomatoes, and some high-energy bars.

It was raining softly when I left my home at 4:30 A.M. Tuesday, November 8. The forecast indicated it would brighten up and would be sunny in Palm Springs. Nevertheless, I took additional clothing, including a poncho.

92

We met at the trailhead at 7:20. Dale's wife came along. She was going to spend time with friends in Palm Springs. She took my van and planned to meet us after the climb at the bottom of the tram between 1:00 and 2:00 P.M.

A hiker should never travel alone. Dale had gotten lost on this mountain on his first solo excursion up the face six years earlier. He had walked out after two full days in the February chill. He'd slept on a rock when it grew dark, and ran out of food and water. The helicopters from the sheriff's department were unable to spot him. If he'd injured himself, he could have died. He stressed to me he was going to be extra cautious this day.

However, Dale had not been informed (nor had he inquired) as to the trail condition. Overgrown and obscured with chaparral and manzanita bush, it was no longer maintained by the forestry service because of budget restrictions.

Additionally, Dale's memory was faulty. We discovered that it wasn't 8 miles but 12. Those 4 extra uphill miles at 500 feet per mile elevation rise take an hour per 2 miles.

One of the major reasons we started early was we weren't sure how quickly Mike would be able to ascend. Don and I normally hiked as a team, having been together for two full seasons, climbing approximately 50 times. We felt confident we could tackle just about any day hike.

Forty-five minutes in, Dale took a wrong turn at a fork in the trail. We lost 25 minutes heading back downhill with no proper marker at the junction. We had to retrace our steps several times as the trail became faint or petered out, losing even more time.

Later, we came to a huge sign that read: "Ranger Station (the top of the tram), 8 miles" and then underneath, in bold letters: "10 hours." We calculated we could climb at least 1½ miles per hour, so we divided it into six hours.

Mike suffered leg cramps and carried insufficient water. Don carried extra water and shared, so he hiked with Mike. Dale and I pushed on ahead, waiting several times for the others to come into view, then continuing up the mountain. We felt confident that even though

Mike and Don's pace was slow, they had plenty of time. It would give us time to mark the trail so they wouldn't go astray.

Short losses consumed more time. We discovered there were three distinct ways to stay on trail: (1) Search for footprints of the people who have previously climbed in your direction; (2) watch for stone or branch barriers made by courteous hikers across areas that lead to dead ends; and (3) follow little stone monuments to point the way placed there by previous travelers. Nevertheless, we wasted 1½ to 2 hours retracing steps and building additional markers to assist Don and Mike.

Time moved quickly. At about 2:00 P.M., I looked up the mountain face and I guessed it would take at least two more hours to reach the top. Now far ahead of our friends, we'd done our best to make sure they could follow our footsteps. It was too late for Dale and me to turn back, as nightfall would come by 5:00. The general rule is that if you're not half way up the mountain by 1:00, you turn around and go down.

We believed Don and Mike were at the halfway mark and would return to base. We didn't realize Don was thinking the way I had. The trail was 8 miles, and by his calculations they would be up well before nightfall. They were continuing up the mountain.

When 4:00 P.M. came, Dale's wife had called the rangers to inform them we'd not come down the tram as planned. Dale had a cellular telephone; I called my office to arrange for someone to take my place for the evening's presentation at the college. We had an hour of daylight left. We were about a 1½ miles from the top and should have been there by nightfall.

This calculation would normally be correct but Dale began to tire, as he was recovering from a groin injury. The altitude was also beginning to affect him. Needing to stay reasonably close, yet continuing to find the trail out of the switchbacks before dark became the challenge. On the ascent, we'd been fortunate because it was also cool. This conserved energy. The lengthening shadows over San Jacinto kept us out of the sun. Dale fell further behind, so I was forced to decide to either hike to the top and then find my way back down to get him (which would be difficult at night), or stay within verbal distance. I chose the latter. This would have been a good time to have referee whistles and a prearranged signal pattern.

Reaching the summit at dusk, I met the ranger. He asked if I was with Dale Lawrence's party. I said I was and that Dale was within a few hundred yards. He asked about Mike and Don. I told him they'd probably turned around and gone back down. He asked how well equipped we were and I told him we were prepared for day hiking.

The ranger escorted us into the tram building and we called my wife to inform the wives of our two friends that they hadn't come out yet, but we fully expected them at the base. On reaching the tram bottom, we jumped into the van and drove to our trailhead, but no one was there. We went back deciding to stay at the bottom of the tram and wait for the results of the ranger's activities.

We became concerned about possible injuries. The rangers decided to sweep the trail from the top, with the sheriff's department coming up from the bottom. At about 9:30 P.M. we received a phone call saying they'd been found within an hour of the top, in total darkness. Don had forgotten his flashlight. Groping around in the dark, they were slowly feeling their way to the top. Our markers had helped, but in the dark it was almost impossible to find the way. The nearby cliffs made the situation extremely dangerous.

The ranger, with his pith helmet flashlight, extra clothes, and water, brought them out. It was on the chilly side—about 30 degrees—when they arrived at the tram, and we celebrated a happy ending.

◆　◆　◆　◆　◆

Always be up to the challenge but take into
consideration the rules and the risks.
There are occasions when the risk is not worthy
of the reward.

DO WE JUDGE
A BOOK
BY ITS COVER?

*"The lust for comfort, that stealthy thing that enters
the house as a guest and then becomes a
host and then a master."*

—JOSEPH CONRAD

The automobile advertisement read "Thinking of You" and then went on to describe the benefits.

...And once your eyes have witnessed the wonder of form and function, and your emotions have been teased by the mystery of its simplicity, you can step inside the cabin and behold a world of sophisticated and ergonomic amenities and prepare for what can only be described as a truly luxurious driving experience.

This inviting message could prompt a customer to walk into the dealership. Imagine the customer's negative reaction if the allure of the ad were dispelled by a sleepy sales representative dressed in a rumpled jacket, soiled Hawaiian tie, and mismatched slacks. Say he's sitting at a desk with his feet resting on top—a visible hole in one shoe—cigar in mouth and reading *The National Enquirer*. To top it off, he's rude because you've interrupted his day. The marketing program has just been mortally wounded.

Or you're traveling late in the evening, tired after many hours on the road, and you spot two motel signs. One is off the next exit, while the other is on the other side of the freeway, more awkward to reach. Your first inclination is to stay at the most convenient location, but you notice a couple of letters are out on the neon sign advertising the motel's name. Now you have second thoughts. If the motel's manager doesn't care sufficiently to create the correct exterior impression, what kind of comfort will you be offered? Will the lobby be unkempt? Have the rooms been vacuumed? Will the shower have water pressure? Will there be enough towels? Are there bottles of shampoo and hair conditioner for extra convenience? Any ice in the ice machine in the hallway? These kinds of thoughts are subjective—however, they're real. You decide not to take any chances and you spend a couple of extra minutes to reach and pay for a night's lodging at the motel across the divide, that has a bright, flawless neon sign.

Impressions, image, and marketing go hand in hand. Our clients "buy" the salespeople as much as they buy the product. We can make poor impressions without realizing it. Even if we know our inventory and give excellent service, we can overlook the seemingly insignificant things that tarnish the image. If your clothes have a sloppy look, it suggests that you're careless about other items. If you pull from your briefcase a shopworn order form or a dog-eared flyer, the prospect believes you're either oblivious to tools that aren't first rate—or you don't give a hoot one way or the other.

Your appointment book or daily planner may detract from the positive picture you're trying to paint. If your notebook bulges with little pieces of paper, it could upset the buyer. What if one of these scraps gets lost and it involves him or her? How about your cluttered car? The children's litter on the seat or the crumbled memos on the floor show a lack of self-pride.

Handing a receptionist a creased business card instead of a clean, fresh one can prevent you from making a good first impression. If I tell someone I will write him a letter as a follow-up to our conversation within 24 hours, I do everything humanly possible to make sure it happens. If the letter arrives later than promised, or is loaded with errors, my personal and professional quality comes into question.

◆ ◆ ◆ ◆ ◆

You do not get a second chance at
a first impression.

ONE HUNDRED DOLLARS PER MINUTE

"Being rich is having money;
being wealthy is having time."

—STEPHEN SWID

Coke-bottle bottoms would aptly describe the thickness of my eyeglasses. I was not comfortable with contact lenses. My solution came through a radio advertisement, a surgical procedure called radial keratotomy. In the early 1980s this was still controversial. Nevertheless, I called their toll-free number.

A warm, friendly voice responded to my inquiry and before realizing it, I had been converted from a curious questioner to an enthusiastic prospect. The telephone operator arranged a clinic appointment the following week.

A warm and friendly receptionist introduced me to the next person in this assembly line. I was guided by a professional-looking nurse, also warm and friendly, and escorted into a warm and friendly room. There sat an extremely large TV monitor and VCR.

Settling down with hot tea and shortbread cookies, I watched intently as a short video explained the surgical procedure, including patient testimonials. It ended with a brief introduction of the surgeon who performed the operation.

Yet another warm and friendly assistant appeared and in a reassuring voice politely asked for the order. I had been impressed by the video display and gladly signed. After I approved the paperwork, she arranged for my return a week later to complete the operation on one eye at a time.

Confident the operation would be successful, nevertheless I chose my bad eye first. Arriving at the clinic, I was escorted into the operating room. Actually, there were two rooms separated by a screen. Two aides were preparing my table. Asked to lie down, I was offered a choice between a teddy bear or a Florence Nightingale doll to hold. I went for the teddy bear.

Without fanfare, the surgeon appeared, also warm and friendly, but he cut (pardon the pun) to the chase. I received a short greeting and a brief explanation of what he was about to do—make small radial incisions around the cornea of my eye. This would cause it to flatten and, he assured me, would dramatically improve my eyesight.

The nurse put a local anesthetic in my eye. Within 15 minutes, the operation was completed—at $100 per minute. The surgeon moved swiftly beyond the barrier to the adjacent operating table where two aides had prepared the next patient. It was like watching a tennis match in slow motion; four moves per hour at $1,500 per move, six hours of operations totaling $36,000. The surgeon had delegated all but the 15 minutes per patient.

◆ ◆ ◆ ◆ ◆

*This was an outstanding demonstration of
the highest and best use of time.*

AUNT EVELYN

"You can outdo you if you really want to."
—PAUL HARVEY

I loved Aunt Evelyn, my mother's youngest sister, from the time I was a wide-eyed small boy in awe of her scary ghost stories to the times I visited her and my Uncle John in my teens. They lived in a small cottage next to a quarry in the Lake District of England where he worked.

Aunt Eve was brought to mind when my assistant, Mary, had the opportunity to see Bette Midler, Tina Turner, and Elton John in concert over New Year's holiday in Las Vegas. She was ecstatic and conveyed to me the magic of the performances. It gave the audience goose bumps. The shows were provocative, charged, hypnotic, colorful, gratifying.

In the early 1970s, my Aunt Evelyn arrived in Los Angeles from the rural community of Threlkeld, a village in northwest England that time forgot. Visiting the United States for the first time, she was amazed by everything—the freeway traffic, the hustle and bustle, the sheer size of the metropolis. We wanted to stretch her envelope even more.

At 2:00 P.M. on a Monday, we flew out of Orange County to Las Vegas, arranging to fly back within 24 hours. A special room had been prepared for Evelyn at the Dunes—flowers, champagne, and a basket of fresh fruit.

We enjoyed the dinner show at the Sands featuring Sammy Davis, Jr., who was sheer electricity on the stage. Then we took a limo to the Hilton, where we caught the late show featuring Elvis Presley, Aunt Eve's absolute favorite.

The next morning Evelyn had a magnificent breakfast buffet and lay around the pool until our departure. For the rest of her life she highlighted this experience as one of her most treasured memories.

In more recent times, I fulfilled two of my goals—to see Frank Sinatra and Barbra Streisand live on stage. I was not disappointed. Both were perfectionists in their delivery and the execution of their presentations. Uplifting, extraordinary, excellently crafted, breathtaking, and masterfully delivered would not be a descriptive exaggeration.

My point? All of these outstanding performers are role models for all of us in sales. On stage they give everything of themselves. The overdelivered and underpromised. They bonded brilliantly with their "customers." Aren't we also on stage? Isn't that a requirement for any real estate agent? Why should it be different for us?

◆　◆　◆　◆　◆

Customers don't buy with logic—they buy with emotion. They use their hearts and not their heads. The best of the best sell the sizzle, not just the steak. Is it possible for each of us to be spectacular, extraordinary, and even exhilarating to our clients—or would that seem too farfetched?

WANNA BUY
A BOOK? WANNA
CATCH A FISH?

*"The world is moving so fast these days that the person
who says it can't be done is generally
interrupted by someone doing it."*

—ELBERT HUBBARD

One day, a young man was selling bibles in Central Park. His whole presentation was, "Wanna buy a book?" A national sales trainer out for a walk in the park suggested if he attended his six-week in-depth course on prospecting he could earn $50,000 a year. The young man replied, "That's great, but I'm earning $100,000 a year now. Wanna buy a book?" No theory for him. In the fast and fickle world of sales, he had found the crowd and was asking for the order.

Doing back exercises Saturday morning at 5:30, I was watching a TV program featuring fishing and hunting. Although not a fisherman, I do enjoy watching how they catch fish. For some, fishing is a lazy sport; for others it's an art and science requiring focus and energy.

The essential requirements for the former are a hook, line, and pole. A worm is good enough for the hungry, undiscriminating fish of a well-stocked stream. The fisherman can bask in a drowsy summer day hoping that some unwary fish will snap the crudely baited hook. On rare occasions, the fisherman is rudely awakened by the fish, perhaps feeling resentment as strongly as he or she relishes achievement—not unlike the salesperson who relies upon customers to come to him or her to buy or sell.

102

The latter fisherman requires reels, leaders, and flies. All equipment is scientifically designed to hook the wary game fish that survived the simple line and pole. The fisherman must be an expert caster and understand the finicky fish appetite. The fisherman must be aware of the seasons and which flies are suited to each one, stalking his or her quarry along torturous courses of brooks and lakes.

◆ ◆ ◆ ◆ ◆

Preparation is power, execution is king.

THE SKIING
EXPERIENCE

*"The great pleasure in life is doing what people
say you cannot do."*

—WALTER BAGEHOT

I had missed my return flight from Reno to Los Angeles; by now it seemed a natural occurrence. Some would call this the trip from hell. For me it was a brief adventure with highs and lows. Three days previously I had flown into Reno alone on Saturday, December 21. I'd originally arranged to meet my ski buddy, Carlos Marquez, at LAX airport so we could take the ski trip together. He'd been urged to stay overnight at my home, but opted to get up at 4 a.m. to take the shuttle directly from his home to the terminal.

He missed the flight; he'd misplaced his electronic ticket and mistakenly thought I'd be at the main ticket counter a LAX and did not check for me at the gate. I'd booked both seats subject to his confirmation and identification, yet the agent at the main counter did not disclose this to him. On returning home from LAX, his shuttle hit a Cadillac; fortunately, no one was injured. We later agreed it was fortunate he'd missed the plane.

I arrived in Reno at 8:20 A.M. I'd arranged for my brother Tim to pick me up to ski Mt. Rose. A snowstorm was coming in, but I wasn't concerned; it would mean powder skiing. No one expected the 8 feet of snow that came in the next 48 hours.

By 10:00 A.M. Tim had not arrived, and I'd discovered that Carlos was safe back at home. At 10:30 A.M. the paging system announced my name. Tim, stuck in a snowdrift, told me he could not reach the airport—it would be shut down due to the extreme weather during the next 48 hours. I shopped for my own four-wheel drive vehicle. Depending on the car rental company, prices varied from $80 to $160 per day. Avis rented me a Chevy Blazer, a four-wheel drive I'd heartily recommend.

Highway 80 west to Sacramento was open. I decided to travel to Truckee and on to the Northstar ski resort 35 miles from Reno. Within 10 miles of Truckee, the freeway signs indicated Highway 80 was closed and I returned to Reno hoping to ski Mt. Rose; however, it too was closed. I'd decided to reach Tim at Tahoe Incline going over the major pass Highway 50, the long way around, but open. It took four hours to travel the 25-plus miles from Reno to Carson City. Autos and 18-wheelers without chains had been abandoned or skidded off the roads. I zigzagged through. Constant stopping gave me the opportunity to read most of a book. From Carson City I started up the pass, almost at the top. A huge hay truck ahead skidded out of control and completely blocked the two-lane highway.

The sheriff arrived; the pass was closed—all traffic had to turn back. Many vehicles lost control and re-blocked the highway. Fellow travelers helped when possible by giving rides and moving vehicles to the side. We caravanned down the mountain in new blinding snow.

Booking a hotel room in Carson City, I grabbed a Chinese meal and saw a movie at the local theater. The next morning the snow had temporarily stopped. So I headed back to Reno up the pass to Mt. Rose since the road had been "cleared" to the ski slopes. The wind was howling along Lake Washoe. It was almost impossible to see. Arriving at the mountain, there were not many skiers. There was just one open chairlift. I skied until 2:00 P.M. When the weather closed in, it became impossible to ski.

Travelers inched down the mountain and arrived at Reno to book a room at Harrah's. I ordered a deli sandwich and watched TV movies in my room. All highways were closed and Carson City was without power. State employees were told to stay home Monday.

Monday dawn broke clear so I skied all day in beautiful sunshine on fresh powder. Small crowds and no waiting lines. After my final run, I called Tim and arranged to meet for dinner at 5:00 P.M. in

Truckee, 6 miles away. What we didn't know was that 267 was the only open road out of Tahoe; traffic was backed up for 12 miles. It took almost four more hours to travel 6 miles.

Five P.M. turned into 8:00 P.M. by the time I reached Truckee. I no longer had thoughts of dinner. The 8:35 P.M. Reno flight was 31 miles away and there were no more flights that night. I arranged a 7:00 A.M. flight the next morning. I stayed at a hotel and requested a 5:00 A.M. wake-up call. I was not going to miss another flight.

The night clerk informed me it could take 15 minutes to get a taxi. What he didn't tell me was that the desk closed down from 2:00 to 6:00 A.M. and the building was locked up. I could not reach information from my hotel room. I found a pay phone at 5:45, the taxi arrived at 6:20, and I made the airport and flight just in time.

Was the two-day skiing worth it? Not to anybody except an obsessed skier.

◆　◆　◆　◆　◆

A competitive, instinctive, determined
drive to complete any and all objectives doesn't
always make sense.

EMBRACING REJECTION

"People learn from their failures. Seldom do they learn anything from their successes."

—HAROLD GENEEN

We all want everyone to love us. A young man seeking to date quickly learns he is going to be turned down—a lot. To win someone's heart he must first embrace rejection. He'll fail most of the time—but not all the time; as his approach improves he learns from his mistakes.

Alfie, the cartoon character, claimed he had never failed. His wife told him he had. His response was he'd never tried, therefore he'd never failed. George Bernard Shaw wrote, "A life spent making mistakes is not only more honorable, but more useful than a life spent doing nothing."

Rejection that is not properly understood as being a stepping stone to success can lead to slumps. We spend countless hours fretting and feeling abused when acceptance eludes us. In the beginning of our sales career, we don't expect such consistent rejection, nor are we conditioned for it, but we experience it. How can we rise to the challenge of meeting new clients and customers if our expectations are not reasonable? If we want to maximize our potential, we have to risk having our necks chopped off and keep a ready supply of glue.

Bonding reduces rejection. A great formula is the use of the acronym FORD, which stands for family, occupation, recreation, dreams. Talk in terms of the interest of your prospect. For instance, "I realize this is personal, but are you a family person? Children? Their ages? Their ambitions: Boys or girls?" (Family)

"I'm just curious, what do you do for a living? How long have you been at it? Do you enjoy your work? Ever thought of making a change? What would you enjoy doing if you had the opportunity?" (Occupation)

"How do you recharge your batteries when you're not at work? What do you enjoy doing with your leisure time?" (Recreation)

"If you won the lottery, how would you spend the winnings? If you put aside some mad money to spend on yourself, what would it be for?" (Dreams)

When I first started selling Gleamy bleach as a preteen, I got rejected 9 out of 10 times. My dad encouraged me by accompanying me to a few doors. He taught me to separate myself from my product. When the homeowner rejected my product, he wasn't rejecting me, and to my delight, they didn't all reject my product.

Prospecting appears to be a lot of effort for small results, but it's definitely not a waste of time. There are other ways to justify your prospecting time. Practice in honing your skills. Outbound phone calls provide badly needed on-the-job training; you become razor sharp, and the effort keeps the adrenaline flowing. Learn your options; predict the types of responses you'll receive. Rehearse, role-play, drill for skill. A script always helps, but the conversation can divert from the script. Prospecting teaches mental agility. You are truly living by your wits.

The script statements should be clearly written. You want to keep the customer talking. They're programmed not to talk to strangers, so they need retraining. A high-structured question will jolt them into talking. In real estate it could be, "Have you sold your home yet?" Or "When are you planning to move?" And "If I could show you a way to own your own home, with little more than rent, would you consider that a benefit?" By asking a question, you're placing the prospect in your control.

The customer might say, "I had no intention of selling my home," or "I don't intend to move," or "I'd rather rent than buy." The next words are critical. There are those that say no in such a way that it really means they're asking for more information. You need to judge who those prospects are. Could they be persuaded or is it really a negative response? If so, reject them before they reject you. You have fulfilled two primary objectives: You reached the person you were trying to reach, and you found out he or she was not interested in what you had to sell.

Dump this customer and go look for someone who wants what you're selling. Why waste time and energy on a person who has told you out front he or she is not a buyer or seller? Dial another number. Not every person you reach will be disinterested. Endear yourself on the telephone. Yes, it's tough. It's easy to get rid of a voice—it's difficult to get rid of a body. Set the appointment to move your body over to the customer to be eye to eye. Rely on your skills; be comforted that those wits will become better with every call made.

◆　◆　◆　◆　◆

Outbound calls make you creative, quick, and resourceful. It becomes fun once you discover that no matter what the person on the other end of the line may be feeling, he or she can't cause you physical pain.

SO WHAT CAN I PASS ON TO OTHERS?

"Americans are like a rich father who wishes he knew how to give his sons the hardships that made him rich."

—ROBERT FROST

Your greatest lessons in selling come with the deals you lose. Those you make only serve to prove the effectiveness of your technique. It's the losses that prompt you to consider your methods and attempts to improve them.

Ideas improve in quality and quantity as we try them out. How many times do we talk ourselves out of a good idea because it meant stretching? There's little hope for the person who lacks the courage of his or her convictions. Successful people are generally very average people who have the courage to try out their ideas.

We all go through a learning curve. It's hard when you've learned enough to realize how little you know. This usually sets in following a period of beginner's luck. You amaze the office and embarrass the veterans by selling an unsalable product at a ridiculous price. Why? Because you don't know any better.

Your walk on the clouds is cut short. You begin to have self-doubts, losing your early effectiveness. You feel a surge of humility caused by your lack of knowledge and begin to despair of yourself and your future as you become increasingly conscious of the magnitude of your ignorance.

In some ways, it's a healthful sign. You understand that you've got to regain control. Open to suggestions, you study. At any stage, you know more about your product than the prospects. That's the consolation. Cherish this thought and proceed with confidence—never confessing your ignorance to anyone.

To master any business requires time and experience. Sales are an intense way to make a living. We can feel the heights of exhilaration, which creates a positive attitude. Yet we can also experience the depths of despondency, which plunges us into what appears to be protracted failure. Learn to stay put long enough to master your attitude and expand your experience. Above all, demonstrate to your peer group and your customer base that you have stability.

We're always in one of three states of mind—a high, a low, or somewhere in the middle. We hit a high when we've found the right product for the customer and closed the transaction; almost there, we drove hard to bring it to a close. Selling requires enthusiasm. If you can't create belief in yourself, it's going to be difficult to create it in the prospect.

No one can stay on a high forever. Nature acts as a pendulum allowing us to plunge into a mental low—the slump—caused by a canceled transaction, a personal problem, or a circumstance over which we had no control. A dreadful experience—it's the penalty paid for the thrilling upbeat moments salespeople enjoy. It comes to us all, but the difference is the length of time and the recuperation period. Some wallow in it for weeks—nursing wounds and grievances. A few never recover and drop out. Others have enough self-discipline to recover. It's not that they feel any less sad or disappointed about the bad breaks; no one escapes those pangs.

The quandary of being somewhere in the middle—in neutral, akin to a coma—is the most difficult state of mind. It very often follows a series of successes. Everybody has left town; you relax, rest on your laurels, and gravitate toward your desk.

It's amazing what happens to our attitude when a sales streak ends. Our minds begin to whisper we just aren't getting any breaks—everyone else is somehow getting all the good prospects. We forget that no prospect is a good prospect until someone writes a contract.

How do you get out of this funk? Take a different route to the office. Make a speech to a local service club. Go up and down a street talking to business owners in a commercial district. Do something different. Action is more important than the nature of the action. Don't let mental and emotional atrophy set in. The key is to force an attitude change and escape the bad effects of a prolonged duration of the blahs.

Come back through prospecting. Keep the following in mind about any prospect with whom you work. First, he—or she—must need the product you're offering. If he does, he's going to obtain it from someone. Let that someone be you. Second, he will eventually buy when he's convinced his need or desire can be affordably met. Third, whether or not the prospect develops a desire to do business depends on your ability to sell yourself. The first two depend on the customer; the third one depends on you.

Adversity is either self-afflicted because of bad personal judgment or a less controllable reason of worsening economic conditions. Fighting adversity requires a sense of urgency and deep-seated belief that the ability to change and self-discipline can correct the problem.

A grizzled sales manager conveys a message from experience to perhaps a young, inexperienced but enthusiastic candidate. A salesperson needs toughness through good times and bad.

He can be a territory pin on a map to his boss, a computer printout to the controller, a pressure point on accounting when his commission is due, a smile and a joke to the receptionist, and a source of goodwill to his customers.

An aspiring salesperson strives for the endurance of Fidel Castro, the resilience of Barbra Streisand, the brass of Howard Stern, the creativity of Woody Allen, the shrewdness of Warren Buffet, the tact of Condoleezza Rice, the charm of Sean Connery, the brain of Bill Gates, and the rhetorical skills of Tony Blair.

Impervious to indifference, cynicism, and complaints, he must be razor sharp after negotiating for hours in a hard chair with an even harder client. He finds the stamina to sell all day, entertain all evening, and show up at the office bright-eyed and fresh at eight the next morning. He must be a good narrator and an avid listener; he must self-debate the decision to be willing to lose in religious and political discussions, or golf and tennis if the situation demands it.

If in real estate sales, he wishes his sellers' homes were priced more realistically, his buyers' offers higher, his fees greater, his prospecting more productive, his competitors more ethical, his escrows quicker, his broker more sympathetic, his advertising more effective, and his clients more human. However, he is a realist who accepts the fact that all of this may never be. Ever the optimist, he makes the sale anyway. He lives or dies by his number of sales posted on the blackboard.

Hours are often used up in a tedium of boring paperwork. A night's sleep can be lost fretting about the one that got away. Nevertheless, each morning the dead weight of yesterday's loss is dismissed and he comes forth with renewed vigor to change the odds.

◆　◆　◆　◆　◆

*Hardships are endured for the financial success
enjoyed; he is absolutely certain that
tomorrow will be better and there is nothing he
would rather be than a salesperson!*

Give the Gift of

Hunger, Hunches, & Hustle

An Englishman's 40 Years of Selling Experience and Misadventures in California Real Estate

to Your Friends and Colleagues

CHECK YOUR LEADING BOOKSTORE OR ORDER HERE

❑ **YES,** I want _____ copies of **Hunger, Hunches, and Hustle** at $12.95 each, plus $4 shipping per book (California residents please add $1.07 sales tax per book). Canadian orders must be accompanied by a postal money order in U.S. funds. Allow 15 days for delivery.

My check or money order for $_____ is enclosed.

Please charge my ❑ Discover ❑ American Express ❑ MasterCard ❑ Visa

Name _____

Organization _____

Address _____

City/State/Zip _____

Phone_____ E-mail _____

Card# _____

Exp. Date_____ Signature _____

Please make your check payable and return to:

Grasmere Press

Cerritos Corporate Towers
18000 Studebaker Road, Ste. 205
Cerritos, CA 90703

Fax your credit card order to: 562-860-2835